T0150393

# NO STRAIGHT THING
# WAS EVER MADE

'These are dispatches from the dark side, from that shadowy land called Depression, but oddly they are illuminating, powerful, empowering. Everyone should read this book because we are never very far from someone who is depressed, someone who is going through something like this. I found myself saying, "Yes, yes, yes" and I found myself crying and I found myself nodding as I read, slowly, savouring it, not wanting it to end and wishing it were over, all at once'—Jerry Pinto, author and poet

'Lucid and wise, wrenching and shattering in its honesty, *No Straight Thing Was Ever Made* explores the homeland of invisible illness through ten remarkable essays on mental health. These beautiful and true essays will change your perception of illnesses and conditions that are so universal, and yet so rarely understood. This is a moving and powerful memoir, a landmark collection of essays and reflections from an exceptionally gifted writer who brings her questioning intelligence to bear on every challenge she faces. It will change your understanding of what it means to live with an invisible, ever-present illness, and to hold on to your deepest sense of self through every bend in the road'—Nilanjana Roy, journalist, literary critic and author

'Brave, lyrical essays, as much to do with coping as with the difficult task of repair. A book we may all want to keep beside us, whatever our relationship with the shadows'—Tishani Doshi, writer, dancer and poet

# NO STRAIGHT THING WAS EVER MADE

ESSAYS ON
Mental Health

# URVASHI BAHUGUNA

**PENGUIN**

**VIKING**

An imprint of Penguin Random House

VIKING

USA | Canada | UK | Ireland | Australia
New Zealand | India | South Africa | China

Viking is part of the Penguin Random House group of companies
whose addresses can be found at global.penguinrandomhouse.com

Published by Penguin Random House India Pvt. Ltd
7th Floor, Infinity Tower C, DLF Cyber City,
Gurgaon 122 002, Haryana, India

First published in Viking by Penguin Random House India 2021

ISBN 9780670091591

Typeset in Adobe Garamond Pro by Manipal Technologies Limited, Manipal
Printed at Thomson Press India Ltd, New Delhi

www.penguin.co.in

*For the therapists who turned my life around,*
*Madeleine who made me stronger,*
*Wendell who taught me to love both Márquez*
*and popular culture,*
*And Aja and Badi*

*For the therapists who turned my life around,*
*Madeleine who made me stronger,*
*Wendell who taught me to love both Márquez*
*and popular culture,*
*And Aja and Badi*

# CONTENTS

# PREFACE

After six years of being immersed in the language of mental illness, coping and recovery, I sometimes forget that I was once someone who didn't know what the various mental illnesses are or how common some of them are. 'Invisible illness' is an umbrella term for any medical condition that is not immediately noticeable by other people. It includes but is not limited to cystic fibrosis, chronic pain, chronic fatigue, irritable bowel syndrome, diabetes and mental illnesses. I did not know what invisible illness was before I fell ill in ways that were unfamiliar and opaque to me.

When I was diagnosed with major depressive disorder in February 2014 (and later with generalized anxiety disorder), it was about a year and a half after I first began to notice that I was feeling poorly mentally and emotionally. In the beginning, in late 2012 and early 2013, it appeared to be a temporary sadness, lack of interest and loss of appetite that I could ascribe to passing circumstances—a break-up; a fight with a friend; exhaustion with the university where classes were routinely cancelled and professors frequently shuffled. But even when those seasons passed, my state of mind remained listless, tired and unwaveringly melancholy. In September 2013, I was leaving for an MA in creative writing in England. I imagined that once I arrived, a new life would replace those feelings with enthusiasm and satisfaction.

Instead, I worsened in the coming months. As the year went deeper into winter, I stayed in bed for most of the day. I struggled to keep up with classwork. I second-guessed myself constantly, wondering if the problem lay within me and whether I had made an error in coming to England. Where I had believed myself to be malleable and brave, I found myself wanting. I was often overcome with anger and fought constantly with my then partner.

A classmate I was friends with recognized some of my symptoms as depression and suggested I visit a general physician at the university hospital. I did not think I qualified as someone who was depressed. I was reluctant to venture anywhere at that time in my life. Deep inertia marked my days. But the hospital was only a couple minutes' walk away, and I finally made an appointment. The physician and I spoke for a long time.

After I was diagnosed with depression and given a low dose of antidepressants, things became just a little easier. I did not know it at the time, but a diagnosis and a prescription were preliminary steps on the journey—not the end of it. It took me from early 2014 to early 2017 to come to a more stable place with regard to managing my depression and anxiety. I had to learn how to better navigate depressive episodes that could last days or weeks and how to more effectively manage the formidable anxiety that could keep me from performing the most basic and necessary tasks such as responding to a work email or showering.

I left friends in restaurants and coffee shops because I could not soothe the climbing anxiety inside me in those moments. I cried at bus stops, in grocery stores, in libraries, on buses and planes. I woke my mother up in the middle of the night because I was physically unable to submit an assignment that I had completed, for fear it was terrible. People around me had to contend with the sudden and substantial dips in my moods and my irrational anxiety. It took time and missteps, and gradually growing apart from some people, to arrive at a new familial and social normal.

In February 2017, I went to an ER because my chest hurt for hours from an extreme panic attack. I had not been on medication for eighteen months at the time. I was proud of that because I thought managing without medication suggested strength and progress on my part. I would give up my medication without consulting a psychiatrist every time I felt better, only to find myself in another depressive episode after a few weeks or months. I felt shame and an unshakeable sense of failure about continuing to experience these symptoms. With a combination of time, therapy, ongoing conversations with informed loved ones or those with similar experiences, and regular medication, I learnt to see my symptoms as the outcome of illness rather than a personal shortcoming, which helped me become far more adept at riding the highs and lows associated with these illnesses.

In part, I wrote these essays because I was surprised by the complexity of recovery—the setbacks, the hit-or-miss success rate of remedies and coping strategies. I had never imagined I would be ill in this way, and I had been wholly unprepared for what recovery would require of me. The determination and stomach for repetitiveness it demands cannot be overstated. Of course, this is not a definitive account of mental illness. It is merely my experience.

I was not, and by no means have become, perfect. Pre-existing flaws, quirks, insecurities and baggage invariably intersect with mental illnesses. They do not cause the illness, but they become carriers for the symptoms. I have written about the way illness permeates every aspect of my life, and I have written about the work it has taken and continues to take to manage my mental health. I have tried to be as real as possible about the challenges while also being hopeful and positive because I have truthfully found both difficulty and redemption on this path.

When I started drafting these essays in 2017, the words were an extension of conversations I was already having with the people in my life. I was trying to normalize for others what I had finally normalized for myself. I explained to them in detail what therapy and recovery involved. I casually mentioned I had a therapy appointment or took my medication in front of them in a matter-of-fact way. I was afraid of their responses, but I knew that we could either live with the knowledge of the illness, or we could grow apart.

In the acknowledgements of her memoir, *Educated*, Tara Westover wrote, 'We are all more complicated than the roles we are given in stories.' This is certainly true of the people in these essays. I will not presume to interpret the text for the reader, but I wish to make clear at the outset that there are no villains in these stories.

This is not a memoir. The essays are arranged thematically rather than chronologically. In these essays, I have written about the way poor mental health has affected my relationships, my work, my decisions and the way I view my body, as well as how I have cultivated and become protective of better mental health for myself. It is important to state that some of the issues and circumstances in these pages may apply to anyone struggling with their mental health—irrespective of what their diagnosis is or whether they have one. I certainly do not want to suggest that mental health is a binary between ill and well rather than a spectrum.

I have used the words 'crazy', 'insane', 'idiot', 'ugly' and 'monster' in reference to myself, to be truthful about how I often felt, in the moments and periods described, before I reached a healthier understanding of illness and myself. Harsh and skewed self-perception is a defining trait of these illnesses. I would not refer to myself or other people with mental illness in those terms in the present.

I have included in this collection two early essays published in 2017 on family and fatigue, with slight amendments to the original text. When I read my essays from a couple of years ago, I am struck by how idealized the family in those pages is, how informed by a moment in time when a wave of forgiveness and mutual understanding had lent everything a soft glow. I was surprised by how outdated, if still true, the poems about my old relationship in my first collection of poems sounded, by how many new notes I have discovered since in that old relationship.

Stories shift. Perspectives mellow, sharpen, become entirely irrelevant. The poet Aditi Rao once told me, 'When

I need to reassure myself, to know that this happened, it was real, I go back to my poems.' For me, revisiting earlier writing is a way to remember that this is one truth, and I may have arrived at a different one, and they can both sit beside one another and be in conversation. In part, I have included these because there is no decisive version of these stories—only a current and constantly changing one.

Working on these essays took more from me than I could have foreseen. It taught me that mental illness is unpredictable and can cause the best-laid plans to be driven off course. I learnt that having unrealistic expectations about my productivity is short-sighted and unfair to myself (and the people I work for). I repaired relationships as a consequence of the questions and realizations that arose while writing and editing. I found that one can love what one does not love all of. Much as I gained, delving into the deeply personal nature of the essays took a toll on me physically and mentally. I asked a long-time friend if she would be willing to read the early drafts and tell me honestly but gently what she thought. I told her I would always warn her when I or the piece were not ready for a certain kind of feedback. These gentle exchanges made the writing of these essays possible. I mention this because care from my community has been pivotal. I put in the work, but support makes the management of my symptoms far easier.

Throughout the time I have been ill, I have had access to healthcare in the form of therapists, psychiatrists and medication. That privilege has protected and restored the health I have subsequently funnelled into working and writing. The education opportunities I have had (including an MA overseas) may not have taught me about mental illness, but they gave me an edge with which to make sense of the illness, the stigma and other repercussions. After the age of fifteen, I have predominantly lived in cities in India that have offered me anonymity, access to good therapists as well as the local transportation required to visit them and flexible work opportunities. I have lived with my family, which has given me the financial security few have. I do not state these advantages to deter those without them from their journey. But I think it is essential to be transparent about what has helped me. Dealing with my symptoms and the balancing of that with my personal and professional life is still tremendously difficult, but I have help.

These essays are not meant to be prescriptive. What works or doesn't work for me may not apply to others. I do not have it all figured out, and lives vary considerably. I am continuously learning and adapting. As I waded through the lowest times, I drew strength from reading material online and in books. There is a list of my recommendations for further reading at the end of the book. There are also notes at the end about the sources I have drawn from.

For those who will read part or all of these essays, I hope they will find a space where they can see mental illness managed and destigmatized. More than anything, I hope to convey that empathy for oneself and others is a vital and achievable skill.

# NO STRAIGHT THING WAS EVER MADE

*On Family*

When I am ten years old, I sombrely inform my mother, 'I'll probably talk to you less and less as I grow older.' She thinks about it for a second. 'No,' she says, 'no, I think we'll get closer.'

~

How does one stay angry at one's family? What does it take away from us? My friends and I talk about family in India. We nurse our grudges close to the chest. We exchange notes, late in the night, about how our parents still make us feel small and disempowered. We crave the soft contours of forgiveness. We pick up presents for them in the places we visit. We fold into those gestures all that is difficult to articulate. We are the ones who glue our families back together. Our parents did not learn that the shortest way to apologize is to say the words. We do not speak the same language as our parents.

I watch one of my friends pull her mother's cheeks after a huge row, calling her, 'my tantrum-throwing child'. The argument washes away. I watch another parcel food for her sibling every time we go out. One drops her mother every week to the airport. This is what we have. In the red-eyed clearing after a bad fight, we consider throwing it all away. In the light that descends day after day, we hold it tightly.

Not because there is only one family to be had in this life, but because their broken ways are our own. Because as Kant said, 'Out of the crooked timber of humanity, no straight thing was ever made.'[1] How desperately we long for our families to be straight.

~

In September 2013, I have just arrived at graduate school in England. It is a windy town, half an hour from the coast. I sob so hard at the end of my first full day that my body shakes as I lie in the sheets of the bed and breakfast on Earlham Road. My mother, who has come to drop me off, asks, 'What is it? Do you miss your boyfriend? Is it the cold? Tell me. How can I leave when you are like this?' We decide I am just overwhelmed, and she goes back home to India. An old friend visits. When she leaves, she sees my face fall, through the window, as her bus rolls away from me. She does not tell me this for three years. When she does, it breaks my heart. I hate that story because it is the story of that entire year.

~

I have a room of my own because my parents want that for me. They have used their hard-earned savings to send me for an MA in creative writing. I am given the life that had never been available to them. My window overlooks a garden with rabbits. My library looks directly on to a lake. I try not to sound sad on the phone. What they do not say is, 'How can you be so ungrateful for the opportunity you have been given?' What I do not say is, 'Why don't you come get me?' My younger sister says, 'You are ruining my chances of being sent abroad for college.' When I cannot muster a smile in my voice, I do not call home.

~

In December, I cannot stop my teeth from clattering. I ask to return home for Christmas. When I do, they say I look completely fine and what was I talking about on the phone from England? What I do not say is that I struggle to write. I struggle to read. My professors suggest too many Andrews, Johns and Emilys to read, and I connect with none of them. I am so anxious I cannot hit send on assignments I have completed. I walk the lit-up campus path near the lake at night. I sleep till noon. *Why didn't you come get me?*

~

A friend at university says I should see a doctor. The doctor has me fill out a form. I have never seen a medical test like this. When my sister and I were little, we would ask, 'What does this word mean?' Our mother always replied, 'Look it up in the dictionary.' In our home, a word means what it means. When the doctor says, 'major depression', my family hears 'very sad but fixable'. It infuriates me when I hear them tell me to try and be happy. But in the stillness of my room, where no one is listening, it is what I say to myself too. Being ill is lonely.

But nothing is lonelier than the first year(s) of trying to explain your illness to people close to you. Once they have understood, the knowledge can sit comfortably in silence. But in the beginning, there are no right words for them to say back to me. Where would they have learnt them? I am explaining something that lies between us and that only I can see. Some have questions. I have answers that I have googled. Some choose silence because they are afraid of saying the wrong thing—perhaps of saying the thing that first comes to mind.

⌒

In 2014, when I move to Mumbai for work, my family has got more used to the idea. But they still offer only the most rudimentary of support and advice. I feel incredibly let down. Why couldn't they have read up? Why didn't care packages arrive in the mail as they did for my friends? Why did other people's parents call every day? I am too upset to admit I would have hated daily calls.

⌒

The TV show *The Affair* shows how different the same memory can be for two people.[2] In my memory, I text my mother saying, *I don't know how I will last another three months at a stressful job*, and she texts back: *Think positively.* We do not speak again for weeks. In her memory, the text conversation is a blur. She was busy and she replied with the advice she had at hand. When I did not respond, she did not pursue. She did not notice that we did not speak because it is not unusual for me to be busy.

In my memory, that night almost breaks me. In her memory, it is a one-sentence text message.

~

Enter a dark room and your instincts must guide you. Do you walk with your arms spread out in front of you? What if you knock something over? If you have nothing but a cache of horror movies you have watched to guide you, how do you navigate the unknown? 'Do not open the door, Jane,' we whisper to the heroine creeping down the stairs to check out that suspicious noise. But Jane does not have a helicopter view of the situation. She is in it, and she must act fast. And sometimes when you see a door and you hear a knock, you cannot help opening it. I thought, *Why the hell did my parents not do better?* But over time, I have found myself suspecting that sometimes one's instincts are not good enough. That is why people die in horror movies.

~

A few months later, in 2015, I make a breakthrough in my mental health journey. An unhappy relationship dissolves. I find a young, hilarious therapist in Mumbai. I pierce my nose (something my ex expressly discouraged me from doing). I get a tattoo, and both my friend and I almost faint during the process. I post these developments on Facebook in a long note about my struggles with mental illness. The response is immense and unexpected. Old teachers, writers I admire and my friends all comment to applaud my 'courage'. It is startling to see how many people believe it is brave. My parents comment saying they are proud of me and support me. But offline they ask, 'Are you sure you want people to know? Won't they judge you? Aren't you afraid of the stigma? What if it affects your chances of being employed the next time around?'

～

Slowly, my parents turn into people who talk about mental health at dinner parties. They are proud of me when I first write about my mental health journey and circulate the article in their close circle of friends and family—many of whom might have blamed their parenting for my mental health issues. It opens a larger conversation within my extended family on both my parents' sides, which allows cousins, aunts, uncles and others to speak more openly about their problems and seek medical help. My sister apologizes for not being there for me and for saying that she thought my illness was holding us both back. The last four years have been a long journey for my entire family. When I point out how differently they viewed my illness in the beginning, they say honestly, 'We did not know, okay? We didn't know.' Sometimes, it is hard to discern whether my pride in my family has completely wiped away the hurt.

～

In this apartment, perched at the top of the building, I am less lonely than anywhere else in the world. In the hallway, my family noisily lets me know their proximity. Each of them has an identifiable footstep and pace. I went to university with a girl who said, 'I have a good life back home, but I don't want to return to it. I want to move on to something better.' I nodded, if only on the inside. When I moved back to this house in 2016, I wondered if it was possible to return and move forward in the same step.

~

Our families' splintered ways of hurting each other mirror their splintered ways of loving. I do not know if people can fundamentally change. But even in their fifties, my parents expanded. They learnt. Does that make it all forgivable? I do not know. I have only learnt to make the questions smaller, my heart a little bigger.

# WHEN YOU'RE VERY, VERY TIRED, YOU CAN'T THROW YOUR TIRED AWAY[1]

*On Fatigue*

'Why do I always hear you saying you're tired,' asks my mother. Trace the word *tired* back to its roots, and you will discover it once meant 'to fail'. I watch my grandmother's body fail in her seventies. Her hands shake when she counts notes for household expenses or reaches for a glass of water with her medicine. She needs a walking stick, then she needs a walker. She stops climbing the sixteen stairs between her floor and mine. I know the body's slow, inevitable failure. My body doesn't fail like that. My body fails in my early twenties.

I have whole weeks where I sleep. I have days where I am tired by noon. All I want is the world's deepest cup of tea to fill me awake. There is so much to do and so much to stay awake for. But there is no reasoning with fatigue. No pleading with my body to fit in one more activity before it needs to rest. I fight with my friends instead. *I can't make it. I know it is early, but I need to leave now. I know I promised, but I have to cancel. I know I'm walking slowly and making us late; I am trying.* There is no other body. There will have to be other friends.

But some people I need to hold on to. Two memories scare me more than the rest. In 2014, I am crying in a hair salon. My sister and mother are getting their hair cut. A hairdresser pulls back my hair into a sink to wash it. I cry because I am *that* tired. I don't want to be in this salon. We are on holiday. My family doesn't do anything else for the rest of the day. I have ruined it. In 2016, I am coming home from a concert, travelling on the London Underground. There is no space to sit. I am too tired to hold up my own weight. My friend leans me against them for the entire train ride home.

When I turn twenty, I fall really sick—for the first time. Over the next two and a half years, two more major depressive episodes follow. But the dissolution of an unhappy relationship and the discovery of a kind young therapist allow me to recover. The frequency of severe episodes decreases. The time it takes me to emerge from them lessens. I still have bad days sometimes. I still have to take care of my mind every day. I have to talk to the knots in my chest, talk them off the edge, help them unravel. My mind has been better since I started taking medication and attending therapy. But my body continues to be tired.

Doctors ask me to run blood tests to check for clues. The pulling of blood into a fat vial, as I see a piece of me leaving my body, makes me nauseous. Three times over, I keep coconut water and lemonade on hand to prevent myself from fainting. All the tests come back clear. I ask psychiatrist after psychiatrist why I want a spoon, a bowl, a whole *dekchi* of sleep. Exercise, they scold. Eat properly, they advise. I want to tell them about the green notebook on my desk filled with lists—foods that decrease energy, foods that replenish energy, foods to elevate mood and so on. But they are already scribbling a prescription for multivitamins. Should I tell them I have three varieties at home?

I finally find a psychiatrist who says, 'How much time do you spend thinking every day? Your mind goes at a hundred miles per hour trying to keep up with all the perceived dangers. Of course, your body is tired. Your sick mind is trying to keep you sad and afraid, while your healthy mind is working overtime to keep you afloat.' I don't have a spike on a blood test. I don't have a name for the doctor's explanation. But it makes sense to me in my bones—that the mind drains the mother ship, that thoughts can tire out flesh and blood.

I come to realize that recovery is a series of loose bolts clattering about inside me—some I have not yet met. If I am to move on, I must make peace with my body. *Have I not already borne my fair share of pain?* I ask those closest to me. *There is no fair share*, I have the task of telling myself. I won't be the young woman in her twenties that my teenage self dreamt of. I won't spend nights at the office outpacing my colleagues. I won't dance at a friend's party until the early hours of the morning.

Instead, I celebrate how many good days there are. I say thank you for all the people who understand why I fall asleep halfway through their dinners. I work from home. I hold my energy close. I choose my friends carefully. Even though my hard work doesn't look like that of my peers, I work hard. I carve out a life that doesn't look like my parents' or like my friends'. I write. There were years (*years*) where the only words I wrote were *I am tired.* I forgive the body.

# EVERYTHING FOR
# THIS BEAUTY

*On Self-Perception, Judgement
and the Body*

# I

I was once cautioned against mistakenly positioning a feeling or mood in the mind or the heart when those experiences were truthfully lodged elsewhere—in the pelvis, upper back, shins and so on. I have a friend who describes her anxiety as a tightly woven knot in the dead centre of her chest. Mine resides in the lower half of my stomach—a pool of water prone to raising waves. It rises (sometimes, I am afraid people think of anxiety as an abstraction without physical attributes). It falls slowly, unevenly, rushing at the end. It isn't stubborn like a knot. Instead, it gains power from the pattern—assault closely followed by retreat, followed by another assault till it settles at an indeterminable point in time, hours or days later.

It quietens as abruptly as it starts up. The larger I am, the more formidable that body of water, the higher it can force the crest of the wave. The worst attacks always run against gravity—surging up the oesophagus, drying the mouth out. The doctor and I often get into disagreements, because he wants to prescribe the medicine that is best for me, but I want the one that won't make me fat. Because the thinner I am and the less convex the stomach, the fewer anxieties I hold.

~

I am engaged, bee-like, in the work of forgetting. Most mornings, when I look in the mirror, I am suspicious of what I see. Ioanna Carlsen was right on the money when she wrote, 'Your fatness always/the one thing you can never believe in/ scales lie/and food vanishes inside you/ like breath.'[1] In the history of my body, I have only inked in the eras of thinness. I cannot be expected to believe the stray photograph that says otherwise. Those that are included next to my poems in magazines are ones taken in the lean periods, ones I can live with. I may not look like that if you run into me on the street.

I don't want the realm of my writing to be invaded with a version of myself that I don't like. The appearance is held to the high standards my writing is held to. I don't want my writing to be tainted.

I arrive at a three-month writing residency with a suitcase full of clothes that do not fit. Was I kidding myself or has my body expanded over the course of an intercontinental flight? Even when I hold fifteen extra kilos inside me, I expect to look like I did three lean summers ago. I look in the mirror, and ask: *Who is that girl?*

## II

Listen, in the beginning, there was a body birthed in the white blue of a hospital room. It was not a good body, though she did not know this at the time. When the body came upon language, she took it for water and drank. But all language is an argument, and it had not yet dawned on the body that she could argue. The story about how she was mistaken for a doll or a white child when she was a baby is a classic. The story about how all the good women characters on television are better looking because they are good people is another staple. When the body learns the workings and temptations of arguments, it is too late in the game. Some arguments have been raging like fires for years. Some arguments become, for better or worse, a place of residence.

In theory, the body is uncomfortable with conversations littered with references to beauty—who has it, who lacks it, who could, who never will. But discomfort is an intellectual position, and there are so many primordial layers that are listening to something else. In hindsight, it has been the work of a lifetime—to fight the form, the shape, the dimension, to learn that no pattern or thought is so complete as the one that daily critiques the body. The body is a vessel that marks and hoards the desire for and the joy of consuming instead of subsuming them into nothing. Mouthfuls that momentarily satisfy and comfort stack up in the body as a sort of criminal evidence, a sort of smirk-revenge by the body.

Listen, a body can stop or start eating for reasons that have nothing to do with hunger or satiation. When the body's parent asks her—for God's sake—to stop eating, she is thirteen, and she stops eating. In under two months, the body will reap the reward when a girl in school will admiringly call her shape an 'hourglass'. That year, and every other year thereafter, the body alternately contracts and expands like something unnatural. Notice that the body has *learnt* the word unnatural. Notice that the body is covered in thin wave lines where the skin has been asked to accommodate change one time too many.

The body is told she won't fit into a pair of export-surplus jeans she wants to buy, and so she contracts. The body is asked if that is fat rounding out through her swimsuit, and the body is too young to know how to contract. Does the man who said that to her remember that it was a small pool, it was late afternoon, she was eleven, and the swimsuit tied at the back?

*Why do I remember this? Is this how I got sick? Did I memorize every experience that felt like a stone?*

The body is advised by a relative to lose weight or she'll lose her boyfriend, and the body tells the relative to shut up and get the fuck out of the house. This is the only time the body swears at or tries to throw out a family member. The body has many regrets, but this is not one of them.

∼

Multiple-choice question: The body has been away from home, i.e. her immediate family, for three and a half months. The body has been on Paxil for a little over a year—an anti-anxiety medication associated with weight gain if used for a prolonged period.[2] The body has been busy writing or having fun or being depressed because of the sunless weather. The body has worked out abysmally little. The body has put on palpable amounts of weight. The body is about to go home and should:

A) Give her family a heads-up that she's put on weight, so they don't remark on it.

B) Give her family a heads-up and specifically request that they don't remark on it.

C) Say nothing. Show up because they are going to remark on it anyway. If she had pre-emptively said something, then the body must accommodate additional anger about her wishes being ignored. If the body says nothing, she must accommodate the knowledge that she did not adequately bolster herself from attack.

D) Give up. There is no controlling other people and no stopping the panic attack because there is no controlling anxiety.

The body went with option B. The body's parent says after ten days, 'I know you said not to ask, but how did you put on so much weight?'

I know you said no, but.

But.

~

Sometimes, a reader who has read some of the body's journey will write to say they are amazed at how forgiving the body is. The body wonders if it is true that people treat themselves the way adults treat them when they're young.

*Is this how I got sick? Did I swallow everything that felt like a stone?*

Perhaps forgiveness was prematurely declared.

~

By way of preamble, the body is told by their sister that she cares about the body. She is telling the body, because she loves her, that the body must lose weight. The sister's faraway friend visits and meets the body for the first time. The friend says, 'You're not fat like your sister said you were!' Everyone laughs, even the body, because it is a great story, and great stories are hard to come by in the realm of body-shaming. They are hard to come by, and the body can't be both fat and humourless.

~

The magical thinking started from the summer of the two consecutive bouts of food poisoning. Boys began to notice the body. The body has cheekbones. One time, her sister notices her visible hip-bones and says, 'Holy shit, those look great.' What else could a boy want? Some weeks after the body returns from a holiday, a boyfriend tells her with a smile that could power up a classroom of hearts, 'You've lost the Calcutta weight.' The Calcutta Weight becomes a thing of luminous, hysterically funny proportions in her imagination. It was two kilos, and it had a name.

*Is this how I stayed sick? Did I start laughing at the stones?*

There is a season where the body is going through its first heartbreak. The body is so thin, it almost isn't believable.

*Do you understand what I am saying? It was like a dream.*

When she is told that she is only skin and bone, she beams on the inside. This is what she has been waiting for. Heartbreak has its upside. The body gets to be thin, which means she gets to be beautiful, which means she gets to wear whatever she wants, attract whoever she wants. Because only beautiful people get to do that, and the body is, briefly, gloriously beautiful.

Over the next two relationships, the body becomes fat. She develops the obsessive habit of asking if it is okay—is she turning the boys off, are they unhappy, does it bother them? She is smart enough to be quiet when boy number one says it doesn't bother him half as much as it bothers her. She focuses on what that says about him—half as much as her is still gargantuan—and after a few minutes of troubling self-realization, lets go of what it says about her. Boy number two says he doesn't think so because he is a tentative person, but the body wants certainty. The body wishes she could divorce love from weight, but she can't.

*I wish I was lying about how much time I have spent wishing for this.*

The hours spent worrying about this would have been better spent on literally anything else. Of all the anxieties, this has been the most time-consuming.

The magical thinking of weight loss went like this—an illness would arrive, and parts of the body would waste away. The magical thinking of anxiety goes like this—always only one more iteration of *breathe in–hold–breathe out* away from releasing it one final time. The magical thinking goes like this: if one wants it intensely enough and with enough of the mind's time, it will happen. An illness will arrive and cut the body in half. Leave rock bottom once, leave it forever. Thin once, thin forever.

~

Accidentally, the body discovers that nothing pulls in an inch overnight like a hard night of drinking. Because the body empties as a response to a signal that analyses alcohol as poison, the body returns to its thinnest possible permutation. Though hungover, the body is relieved once the worst of the vomiting and headaches is over. The body thinks the morning after is the first day of a fitness plan that will fix everything.

This does not happen.

*Each wave of surprise surprises me.*

Let's indulge in some math. The body says 1) she will change many times a year, 2) the body hates herself every day, 3) but the body only changes once every couple of years. What is the ratio of inertia to change?

In a spirited sprint—adrenaline breeds adrenaline—the body sheds five, ten kilos. It feels good, it feels like this will last—is there a better feeling in the world than the one that suggests a good feeling will last? This is the body that could go on forever. This is the body she will die in. The body reads Kaveh Akbar's poem, 'Every Drunk Is Trying to Die Sober, That's How We Beat the Game'.[3]

Will the body die thin? Will the body beat the game?

~

The body is told by a boy that eating well is about health, about living longer and better, about better mental health. The body agrees—what is not to agree with in something so reasonable? The body would like some beer and bar snacks, please. The body is aware of the implicit criticism in the lack of such an order by the boy. What does this boy without complexes or fat or a desire to eat past one's feelings know about hunger anyway?

~

In this season, work deadlines are intense, and a man has taken to harassing the body to the point she cannot stomach any food—until the body is eating an Alprax a day. Then it is a beer a day, and the body is angry when anyone tells her to stop because anyone should be grateful it is just one beer, anyone should be grateful the body isn't drinking themselves beyond the limits of human reason, beyond the point where aggression can be suppressed. What do they know of the debris left in the wake of truly bad drinking?

This is nothing.

~

In the summer of heavy antidepressants and mood stabilizers, the body bloats. The body is aware that the end of that sentence in her head is '. . . like a whale', but she is trying to seem gentler than she is. For a while, the body has the luxury of living in a city that isn't the well-dressed capital; she wears ballooning clothes and tells everyone that it is part of her new, freer self. Everyone nods along and says, 'You look sooo much more like yourself.'

The body is unaware that substantial weight gain is accompanied by a shift in breast size. The body develops ugly welts beneath her breasts because the bras no longer fit, and the underwire has been steadily carving crescents into her for weeks now. The welts are just short of open wounds before she thinks to change. The body realizes that even her undergarments now need to account for her volatility.

The body buys a white dress because one boy likes white, but when she puts it on, she and the boy can tell it was an aspirational purchase. The body barely fits into the dress and must take it off to put on more appropriate clothing before she leaves the house. Notice the word 'appropriate' rolls right off her tongue. The body is size 2, but also the body is 4, 6, 8 . . . but the body cuts off the Medium and Large tags before anyone can see them. The body reads the sizes in the system with the lower numbers to think of herself as a smaller size. The body is obsessed with the body.

~

Where are all the hit songs about people who dream of thinness as much as they dream of anything else?

~

The body, in withdrawal from medication, takes to a steady internal screaming at herself. The body is the worst-looking body in the world. The body is so ugly that the body avoids every mirror and camera flash. Three photographs survive from this time, all to do with work—unavoidable. The body sees them in her head, clear as day as if they were from her wedding day or graduation. The body recoils in horror at those memories. At the school where she works, the body's students tell her by way of reassurance that she is neither too fat nor too thin, when they see her eating only a little at lunch. The body's older colleague tells her by way of a compliment that she can tell from the body's bulging weight that she must be very happy, and the colleague is happy to see that the body is happy. The body's aunt says—before hello—that the body has never looked better. The body is growing loopier by the day. The body and the mind seem indivisible, inseparable by now. The mind is in the stomach, railing at the blubber.

The body gets a tattoo because the body thinks that if she tattoos a message on her wrist, it will serve as a permanent reminder to be kind to one's self. Needless to say, the body is an idiot. The words are supposed to conjure maternal feelings towards herself—love thyself, vessel and all, warts and all. But the body just stubbornly goes on wanting to be thin. The body changes its screensaver to read: *Things take time, so just have patience.* Black background, white text. This works slightly better—we look at our phones more than we look at our hands.

When everything is going well, the body is still the body—still *with* the body—and even an accidental sighting of its shadow or reflection in shop windows will remind the body to hate herself. And the body doesn't argue, doesn't hesitate; she knows what to say, the familiar places to enter the knives. When the body's mother tells her that she goes from crisis to crisis without a breather, the body laughs a little on the inside. The mother doesn't know that the bridge between each real crisis is populated with anxiety about the body—how hateful the body she has inherited is, how hateful the body medication makes is. But the body spares the mother those lines. The body doesn't say she thought she would never mimic the shape of other women in their family. It is unspeakable. Older people's bodies provide the ultimate illusion—not age's inevitability but a cautionary tale. Notice how the road to lifelong anxiety is paved with hand-picked illusions.

*Is this how I stayed sick? Did I choose illusions for ambitions?*

The body loses her shit in the middle of the street at her date, who is dumb enough to take a bad photograph of her. How dare they not ensure they made her look thin or camouflage her? The body melts down. What are the notions of female fragility and preoccupations with appearance women are supposed to resist? Somebody please remind the body. Anxieties about appearance are held over tripwires that connect patriarchy and feminism, and somehow the body is falling short of the standards of both.

Some feminist acquaintances are aghast when she says blithely that she is fat and ugly. 'She is putting herself down,' they say. The friends roll their eyes and tell her she is neither, which is the right answer. She doesn't want to be feminist as badly as she wants to be told she is thin.

The date quietly throws away the polaroid that the date loves on their quiet walk back as the body seethes and cries and takes the SOS medicine, which will turn her into less of a monster. The body is grateful the photograph is in the bin, even though she doesn't say so. She never wants to allude to that evening again, and she definitely never wants to see that photograph.

The date is disarming in that he perseveres. No one who knows the body is stupid enough to keep taking photographs of her when she is furious at the photographs, at the body she doesn't recognize within the photographs. But he takes them and loves them and organizes them into piles. He wants to remember these, he says. The body is shocked. Remember her as she is now? She's certain these photographs are better taken when she has lost the ten kilos she is always telling herself she will lose. She learns to stop looking at the photograph. She only needs to see them once to remember the protrusion of her thighs, the round swing of her behind that takes up what she thinks is most of the photo. She has panic attacks from these photographs; she gnaws at these images as she stews in her anxiety every night. When she doesn't see them, she is almost peaceful. She is almost happy someone loves her enough to keep photographs of her.

~

Anxiety is a blue pool the body swims laps in.

There's anxiety that's locked within one's self, and there's anxiety that travels through one's hands. The body takes to nervously touching her face over and over to help soothe her obsession with external imperfections. It is not until the body learns of a girl who shaves her head—because she can't stop picking out her hair—that she realizes that what she has fits neatly into a subset of obsessive–compulsive and related disorders.

Over time, the body can't help but do this in front of other people, not just her sister—and siblings are a kind of shadow anyway. Her sister begins to worry. 'Can't you tell where you are when you're doing it any more,' she asks. When the body's mother says, 'Don't do that', the body freaks out. No one is supposed to know about this, no one is ever supposed to mention it. How could the mother make the body sound so weird, so strange, so insane? She tells the mother to not ever talk about it again. She knows her friends might notice, but they never say it and that is partly why her friendships have survived. She knows that anyone looking out of the side of their eye could have seen her. There are days she leaves the face so red, she scares herself. She slaps herself, as if that will return the face to its normal colouring. The body doesn't look in the mirror for a while; she tries not to touch it on a day she knows she must meet other people. She hasn't worn make-up before, but she buys concealer, foundation and a colour corrector to start hiding the marks from people.

Most of all, the body hates it when her mother asks her if she's been doing it again.

∾

Ali Akbar Natiq writes a book of short stories and calls it *What Will You Give for This Beauty?*[4] The body wants to turn that purple book cover into wallpaper. She doesn't need to read the book. What would she give? Anything, everything. She would give money and time—she has given so much time. The doctor says, 'Look at your level of emotional pain, and your primary concern is that the medicines that will make you better will also make you put on weight?' 'Yes,' the body says. Yes—she'd only be imbibing future anxiety. She is angry that thinness is not the answer to a prayer, not a mercy for the obsessed.

## III

There is an entire genre of titles that are variations of 'The Weight of'. Anything to which a weight can be ascribed—objects (Anne Michaels's *The Weight of Oranges*), natural phenomenon (Mariah Dietz's *The Weight of Rain*), abstractions (Marianne Fritz's *The Weight of Things*), tastes (Li-Young Lee's *The Weight of Sweetness*)—has been tacked on to this title format. It is embossed on the covers of everything from fantasy (David Dalglish's *The Weight of Blood*) to literary fiction (Rachel Kadish's award-winning *The Weight of Ink*) to religious essays (C.S. Lewis's *The Weight of Glory*). It is an effective naming tool—weight with a capital W lends gravitas and profundity. It refers not only to the solid nature of things but also to their essential cost. Everywhere, except on the body, weight is a thing that moves people. On the body, weight isn't that grandiose, isn't open to extended metaphors. If Atlas had been asked, he'd have scoffed at the idea that rain and sweetness have a weight he could have felt on his back. Human weight is the opposite—undeniable, visible, measurable—like telling time, and about as interesting.

In the sea of throwaway remarks about my appearance are several people who love me and whom I love. Some people certainly didn't want the best for me, but largely, the remarks have been without malice. Or without malice that originates with them—it is an inherited and unchecked network of remarks that leads people here. If I were to break ties with every person who's contributed in small and large ways to an exhausting, time- and soul-consuming anxiety, there would be no one left. Several years ago, one of my friends said carelessly that I would be beautiful but for my nose. It caused a wave of laughter from the other people in the room. It upset (I think) both of us. I'm still friends with her, and we share exasperated stories about the unkindness of relatives for whom our bodies will never be exactly right. Another friend once joked that bikinis were not meant for girls like me. I have often thought about that remark and failed to reconcile it with someone who has supported me through more panic attacks than I can count. The remark was made almost a decade ago, and we've never had run-ins like that again. He was kind when people made loud note of my medication-induced weight. He told me firmly to tell people it was from medication and to lay off. I have found staying the arc of long relationships shows me who's willing to evolve with time. I am, after all, a very difficult person in my own right—hardened and immovable in so many ways. In the past, I have been reckless and unkind in how I have spoken about another person's body. I have had my own trespasses, my own meanness that needed forgiving by someone else.

~

I find stories about hating one's body often end in one of two ways—with correction or with acceptance. What happens to the stories without either? Carmen Maria Machado wrote about her body, 'I do not hate my body, because such a thing would be pointless, short-sighted.'[5] But myopia draws strength from the consuming nature of what is right in front of you. The idea of my body as flawed and in need of rectification consumes me till I cannot see past it. Pointless and short-sighted are pale arguments in the face of that. Repetition is a language all on its own. Being stuck is a language all on its own. I wish I could pretend that I will not worry about this in the future, that complete catharsis is closer. But the most I can hope is to cohabit this body with anxiety better. I have learnt to have more than one voice inside me. When the anxious voice speaks, I ask, as Rilke suggests, '[A]s often as it wishes to spoil something, why something is ugly.'[6] I wrestle with the other voice for the wheel, day after day.

~

# TWO DEER IN THE HEADLIGHTS

*On Dating with Mental Illness*

He and I grew up in the same state, on different sides of the Mandovi River, approximately seven kilometres away from each other. I remember the day I met him. We went to the best school in the northern half of the state (overlooking the sea), affordable enough at the time that a wide spectrum of middle-class families could afford it. We came up around the same small-town failures and claustrophobia—clannishness, rigid gender binaries, homophobia, little to no inter-religious relationships or marriage, with the terror of gossip and the stake of one's reputations constantly drilled into us. Most people we knew were smart, but sheltered and shuttered like us. We knew respectability was not an antiquated need for most people around us, and that stigma and judgement were a stone's throw away from where any of us stood. Leaving the state, however briefly, was a rite of passage for each of us, pushing at the boundaries of ourselves, stretching out what we knew of the world.

When I fell ill, we were two well-educated twenty-year-olds, who had watched a great deal of Western television and movies without stumbling upon these issues, and who thought of themselves as liberal and well-informed. We had known each other for more than a decade. We had a shared childhood of reference points and social markers. As far as we knew, we were good people who expressed empathy and solidarity in tough situations. In this one, we found ourselves completely at sea. It was the coincidence of being in a British university during my illness that led to a classmate correctly deducing that I was depressed and sending me to a doctor. But after I was diagnosed, I baulked at the idea of being depressed, recoiled at the thought of telling people about it. Caregiving to both of us was sitting by someone's bedside, usually an old person, keeping them company and running errands. But those had mostly been our parents' roles, our turns had not come yet. I felt deep shame when I heard you had told your mother I was sick. I assumed that meant I had shifted in her mind from a safe choice to a compromising one.

~

When we broke up, I told my parents over the phone. My father broke into song. He sang the first two bars of a melancholic Hindi song from the 1964 movie *Sangam*, with glee, over the phone while my mother tried to shush him and express some more suitable words of comfort. But all I remember is the sound of my father's happy voice singing, '*Dost, dost na raha, pyaar, pyaar na raha.*' *My friend is no longer a friend; my love is no longer my love.*

One of my clearest memories of my father is his habit of singing ridiculous lines from melodramatic songs to mark moments—family gatherings, weddings, victories for India in international sporting events. That song was all my father had to say about the conclusion of a twenty-eight-month relationship that had spanned a graduate degree, a first job, two displacements. For once, my father's lack of diplomacy made me laugh. No one was wasting breath pretending that our separation could be considered a loss.

∽

The night we broke up, one of my closest friends said to me, 'You can spend the same amount of energy on trying to salvage this equation or on getting over him.'

So, I chose where to spend the little currency I had left.

∽

It is strange to realize that we fell in love when we thought I was mentally healthy, when for all visible purposes I was the definition of sane and stable, and a source of comfort and easy happiness. In times of sickness, we drew on those memories and the emotional wealth and solid foundation of those early months. We had been together eight months when I noticed I was falling apart—needing you with a keenness I hadn't before, crying every single day, racing home from class to collapse into bed and reach over phone lines to you. Sometimes, I called you on the walk back from class. You would pick up, often surrounded by friends, and my anger would light like a match into flame. You knew what time I got out of class; why couldn't you clear time in your day for me? There was little room for reason in my mind.

Sickness midway through our relationship redefined who was needed by whom, and how much. The relationship was no longer what either of us signed up for. 'I don't know how it got this bad,' was one of the messages you sent me early on in the deterioration. I recognized in your voice the same measure of bewilderment I felt—how two happy individuals became so unhappy in a matter of weeks, how things fell apart so rapidly. 'You were the one thing I thought I could count on,' I said in a different conversation. But by then, all our conversations had settled into a pattern of need and resentment, mirroring each other in growing intensity.

In the documentary *Unrest* (2017),[1] a woman named Jennifer Brea falls debilitatingly ill shortly before her wedding. A doctor takes her fiancé into another room and says it is okay to leave her. That story makes me angry, but pragmatically, I knew I was not who I was at the start of the relationship. I knew I had become grittier, angrier, moodier. A part of me acknowledges that people are allowed to leave when the people they are with change fundamentally. The illness changed my moods and behaviour first, and then slowly who I was and what mattered to me. Some studies indicate that 75 per cent of couples dealing with chronic illness separate.[2] A study in 2009 showed that following a diagnosis of cancer, a marriage was six times more likely to culminate in divorce or separation if the wife was the patient.[3] It took a long time for you to leave.

~

For most of our relationship, I was sick. Sickness is definitionally a loss of time, of productivity, of visible output, of money. Lying in bed when one is supposed to be in class or at work, or studying, reading, writing. Stationary when one could be growing, looping the circuit of obsessive thoughts when one could be with friends, looping the circuit when one needs sleep. Waking up tired when all one appears to do is sleep. In my most depressed semester, my final score was one of the lowest in the cohort. I knew the ten poems, the basis of that score, were substandard when I turned them in. I delayed submitting for as long as I could. I had to force myself over nausea and panic to hit send. I bailed on a visit to my closest friend in the country at the time. I took the bus towards her. At the changing station, I got off and went home. She had already bought ingredients for the meal she would cook for me—prawns and greens, my favourite. I told her I had food poisoning. A couple of years went by before I explained I had sobbed hysterically on the bus towards her, sobbed hysterically on the bus away from her, but that my body wanted to go home, wanted to arrive at the house of a friend who already knew how sick I was, who wouldn't crumble in shock and worry when she saw me. This was how it was for a while—bailing on friends and family, poor writing, average work for my part-time employer.

Unhappy relationships too are a drain on time, emotional resources and stability. Waiting for responses to texts and emails became a task in itself. Seething at the small injustices of neglect and the emotional withdrawal of the other person was how I spent much of my time. The problems in the relationship eclipsed every other priority in my life. Perspective is a distant dream when one's mind is good at one thing—latching on to an obsession. It did not occur to me that I could pursue my own life while I waited for you. When it did occur to me, I still held fast to my habits, no matter how self-destructive they were. I did not know when the text, the email, the call would come. So, I stayed stationary. I held my breath. For most of our relationship, I was profoundly unhappy. Yet I needed you, because even the unhappy familiar was better than the unknown when I was depressed.

Because you were the person I already spoke to every day, you were the closest to my illness. I was too confused, embarrassed, conflicted to tell my friends back home. You were part of the day-to-day, minute-to-minute survival. But in all that time, I had not had a moment where I thought, this person is a part of my recovery. The depression and our relationship were a chicken-and-egg conundrum. No amount of therapy has helped clarify which made the other worse.

Some well-meaning friend told me that it would take me at least twice the length of time I had been in the relationship to recover. But I had already lost too much time that I could have spent growing as a young writer or at my first job. I could not afford more. When we split, I spent the next two years throwing myself back into everything the sickness and the relationship had kept me from.

For the first year after we split up, I went to workshops and writing retreats. Everywhere I went, I described my life (in essays, poems and free-writes) in a 'before' and an 'after'. It was how I thought of myself—half in the before (still defined by being with you) and half in the after (still figuring out all the possibilities that being without you opened up). What I learnt in the first months after you was invaluable to my mental health, to my recovery, to the construction of an evolved self. I do not believe that pain necessarily serves a purpose, but in this context, it pushed me to fight harder for myself. I learnt to stop seeing myself in absolutes. I understood anew what my priorities needed to be. I knew I needed to leave the development sector to return to writing, to move home, to reinvest in my female friendships.

Once you left, it took me a week to unspool from my dependency on you. Seven days of coming home without the promise of an admittedly fraught but dependable phone-call. Seven days of replacing that call after work with a glass of port wine (one hundred and sixty rupees a plastic bottle for Port Wine 1000) and a second bath was all I needed to know I was never going back. The space to discover this had finally been provided, and I was grateful.

The inability to leave an unhappy relationship is linked by researchers to the 'sunk cost fallacy'—an irrational decision based on past investment because we do not want to acknowledge a loss. We focus more, behavioural economists explain, on what we stand to lose than what we stand to gain by walking away. Writing about loss aversion, Daniel Kahneman said, 'When directly compared or weighted against each other, losses loom larger than gains. This asymmetry between the power of positive and negative expectations or experiences has an evolutionary history. Organisms that treat threats as more urgent than opportunities have a better chance to survive and reproduce.'[4]

The depression magnified the need for love, if that makes sense. It gave the love a higher decibel, a more resolute form. It made me fear being alone, being without the familiar—even if the familiar was a knife turning inside me. I remember all the times I almost left, threatened to leave. As Ann Patchett wrote, '[T]hey broke apart and came together so many times they were like a plate that had been dropped on the floor repeatedly: more glue than china.'⁵ After witnessing my multiple threats of leaving followed by inaction, my mother finally got exasperated and told me, 'You do not have it in you right now to go through with a break-up. Just leave it be.' She was right. I only had strength enough for threats. The truth is, I needed you to leave. I could trust another person's decision, another person's judgement as final, as the right decision.

You were overwhelmed sometimes by the depth of my need. 'Care a little less,' you said. 'What is one missed phone call?' you asked. *Less*, you pleaded with me. I could not be less needy, even though I tried. The request to be less myself had different outcomes. I become less political, less outspoken, less confident. Because I was shrinking, I held fast to the relationship as a kind of a lifeboat. The anxiety kept me on the threshold of leaving, unable to get my feet out the door.

I was in limbo for months. You leaving me cut me loose.

Katy Maxwell wrote, 'You must allow yourself to outgrow and depart from certain eras of your life with a gentle sort of ruthlessness.'⁶ But departing is not simple, because crazy leaves a trail. Crazy cannot be denied, same as a sloppily executed crime. You told me, 'Do not act as if I alone hurt you; do not act like you did not hurt me.' You threatened to pull up all our emails and show me how crazy I was and how difficult I was to deal with. You installed a software that allowed you to see how many times I checked your social media. You were so angry. You demanded to know why I checked it almost every day. I tried to explain that I just wanted to keep up with your life. I just wanted to be close to you. You were not buying it. This was more proof I was crazy[7] and *controlling*. In the first year of my depression, I want to be clear—I was completely out of control, I was unstable and unhappy in a way that made everyone cringe. I am sorry I looked at your social media, sorry I wrote you long emails that you could pull up as proof of how deranged I was.

~

In what would be the last six months of our relationship, I moved southwards towards plantation coffee and humidity. Towards single tickets to movies. Partly so that I could be in the state next to yours. The distance reduced to a fifth. You visited once. On my birthday, you asked your friend to take me out. He steadied me. He kept a small bottle of honey and lemons in my apartment. He always carried a 50-ml bottle of whisky on the evenings we hung out. In the city where I had moved to be close to you, he became my platonic, loving home. Once, during an anxious spell, I could not remember if I had left the iron on, and I was several hours away from the apartment. He took his spare key and checked for me. In those months, he was the heaviest of my anchors. He was a foil for you, a reminder that neither love nor masculinity had one mode alone. I walked to the sea in the midst of a panic attack, and he stood there with me for an hour, even though he had places to be. You said you had places to be. You said that I did not know all the sides of your friend. But he was my friend by then, and his sides—busy, hustling in a competitive city—were still there for me. When I left the place, his family gifted me a set of wine glasses I still hold on to.

When I drink from them—sometimes something as innocuous as orange juice—I think of how it needed ten times the love to dig me out of one person's neglect. How sickness is exasperating in its need for more attention, patience and tenderness. How it demands that when the person is weak, without a lot to offer in return, when they are not easy to be around. This would become a pattern in my illness, with my friends taking me in, making space on their floors, in their spare bedrooms, their sofas, even their own single beds, sharing the one pillow and blanket they had in their dorm room—sleeping together head to feet, feet to head.

After it was over, but still fresh, my therapist asked me to imagine you were seated in the empty chair next to me. She asked me to address you. Later, she asked me to switch chairs and respond in what I imagined to be your voice and your words. I do not remember what I said—only a concerted effort to sound balanced. I remember the movement between the chairs; the impression that we were speaking to each other in a controlled setting, where the possibility of it spinning out of control didn't exist; the idea that what needed to be said could be said without you. I made your tone and words drift between concerned and trying to do your best, and frustrated and cruel.

Even now, I do not know if this was a disservice to you.

~

I found a note I scribbled at the time that exemplifies the degree of conflict I felt. I had written, 'At night, I compare myself to men who beat their wives.' Was my insistence abusive? Was my neediness harmful to you? In my mind, my clamour was a din in your ears, even when you covered them with your hands.

Even if it was the illness, the teeth were mine. They were attached to a well that sprung undeniably from within me.

~

One of the two pieces of luck I may never recover from is that I found my therapist a few weeks before we broke up. She seemed almost relieved for me when I told her we had split up. She shared that the first time I had told her about us, she had made a mental note: *This relationship is going to take a lot of work to fix.* The other piece of luck was that we broke up in the first week of April—the month where poets around the world sign up to write a poem a day for every day in April. I only wrote nine poems in those thirty days—but it was more than I had written in a year.

During my time with you, I wrote extraordinarily little outside of writing to you. The words had to be pulled out of me just so I had enough poems to submit the dissertation needed to pass my graduate degree. During that time, my writing was predominantly in the form of texts, emails, letters—to you. I kept a notebook, where I collected quotes that reminded me of you. In there were the opening lines of Sylvia Plath's poem 'You're': 'Clownlike, happiest on your hands, feet to the stars.'[8] One of my only poems from that time that I deemed worth saving read, 'You are a slow piece of shark tooth digging into my rind.' I remember those two, and I have forgotten the rest.

In April, my life turned a corner. At the time of our split, I was in the very early stages of recovery. I had a therapist to lean on. I was writing, which meant that I believed I could keep writing. It was as if the other spheres of my life were waiting to grow in the space you left. The writing I did in those months brought to the surface the first raw bits of my healing. That writing became the ramp I used to get far away from us, away from that moment when you told the writer when she was depressed that she was mechanical, lacked spontaneity and needed to be more creative.

I read an essay recently by Elizabeth Weil, about her daughter, Hannah W. Duane.[9] The essay included annotations from Hannah, who pointed out all the details she remembered differently, all the things her mother thought she had been thinking that she had not. I know you have notes for me, places where you do not agree with this version of the story. I used to not be okay with that. I used to feel that surrendering any power to you, even the simple power of telling a parallel tale, was too much for me to bear. Sometimes, your proximity is enough to make me feel less real.

Months after we broke up, you asked me how I was. When I said I was well, you replied that you knew me, knew I could *not* be good. I cried for hours. I almost believed I was not getting better because you decreed it. That is the power you held over me once.

Two years after our split came the worst of my panic attacks. You were in town. We met up with common friends for a drink. I drank too much and the next morning my body fell into a deep, deep panic. It took me a few hours to realize that my body was screaming at me for drinking around you, for letting my guard down around you. I took myself to the hospital where they finally managed to calm me down. My chest and ribs hurt for days after.

I have learnt my anxiety rises like bile at what it cannot tolerate, what it perceives as signs of imminent danger— travelling, missed calls from my parents, unread emails, crossing roads, climbing thin mountain paths, you. The truth is that while in my mind I have recovered, the fear remains that depending on someone the way I depended on you could take it all away from me again.

~

Sometimes, I have a dream where some terrible event befalls you, and I must reckon with the things I have not said. Usually, in the ensuing reunion, something like friendly reconciliation comes to pass. After all, I remember the day

I met you—seventeen years ago—like it was yesterday. But in the realm of sickness and caregiving, forgiveness feels like too simple or too vulgar a concept. It seems to imply that after bad things happen—small and large—love, apologies and forgiveness are currencies to be exchanged. Sometimes, I cannot bring myself to be that transactional, to admit in my forgiveness that some petty part of me still believes there is a debt to forgive at all.

⁓

Partly because we're taught to set more store by romantic relationships than any other, partly because you were the person closest to me through my sickness—I expected the most from you. Even though we had all groped around in the darkness . . . my family had been unprepared, my friends too. I could not at the time, and for a long time after, extend the same fallibility to you. The romantic relationship is privileged in the collective imagination over other kinds of relationships—it is supposed to make us whole, to possess comforting powers of longevity.

I don't think I ever told you that when I was sad over you for some reason or the other, resentful that you did not do more to take care of me when I was depressed, my mother referred to you as 'a young man'. I remember that expression because she was trying to bring home to me the realization that you were as young, as clueless, as unequipped as I was for the situation we had found ourselves in. Being with you exposed my fault lines and limitations. It showed me the naivety of depending overwhelmingly on one person for comfort and release from a serious illness. I have come to understand our failures as part systemic, part inexperience. Looking back, I see us as not what we could have been, but what we were—two deer in the headlights.

~

# BUOYANCY

*On Writing*

# I

S and I met the way the lucky ones do. We walked from different worlds into the same classroom and shared it for the three years it took to graduate into early, sheltered adulthood. We both wanted—nakedly but quietly—to write, to study writing, to pursue it in some shape or form, though I don't believe either of our lives has been governed by that impulse alone. It has been eight and a half years since we met, since I suggested that the college library's copy of *The Yale Anthology of Twentieth-Century French Poetry*[1] might be worth checking out.

Towards the end of our college years, I did not immediately return to class after the winter break between 2012 and 2013. It was the beginning of the depression, but I did not know it then. She called after a couple of days, appalled at my absence, asking if I had decided not to come back. I was jolted into returning to classes for a couple of weeks. But I showed up for very little of the rest of that final semester, read none of the required texts, scraped by in my exams so that the hard-gotten grades from the previous two years could barely assist in reaching an average of some academic dignity. Having applied to graduate school before I dipped, I got in on the strength of an application I had made when I was healthier.

After our undergraduate studies, we both proceeded to study writing at different universities. S settled into independence, growing a voice that was about the quietest parts of living, writing poems that showed a tentative but deep understanding of people and the fragile connections between them, essays that were about what lies beyond the mere one or two languages many of us hold. All the while, I wavered under lengthy bouts of depression. The desire to write, to do anything but lie in bed, ebbed away. When I did manage to put my resistance aside and attempt, I found I did not have anything to say except—I am tired, I am tired. The wisdom, with writing, is that one must write from one's core. But what lay at my core at the time was anger, fatigue and profound reluctance.

In graduate school, S was (from a distance, because, for a time, I held myself at a distance from everyone) tireless—tireless in taking walks when she was by herself, reading every poet on the university shelves, writing, writing. From time to time, I flip through my graduate-school notebook. Far from filled to the brim, it holds paragraphs and diagrams copied from books on oceanography (science being a sturdy shore far away from the poems I wasn't able to write), false starts to poems about the relationship I was in, sentences about needing sleep, words that make me think: God, I was once so young and lost, and there isn't enough money in the world to compel me to go back to that time.

Because I was twenty-one or twenty-two, because S and I had for four years closely resembled one another—even as she emerged as the responsible one, and I as the impatient and inconsistent one—because I had not considered the ways in which timelines do not run parallel in perpetuity, I watched her write steadily, publish, win awards, and I thought perhaps my unhappiness at a time in my life where I was meant to be writing was a sign that writing wasn't for me. I saw S not as a healthy contemporary, but proof that I was not, after all, meant to do what I had grown up believing I would.

I shifted towards another career, a simpler one in terms of pursuits and goals. I worked in non-profits in the fields of education and women's rights. I watched movies and read crime novels, moving away from writing even in my free time, towards unthinking distractions. There was a man in the Pali Naka vegetable market who sold pirated DVDs—I was a regular customer. It was as the writer Paige Cooper said about watching American football, 'I'm reading this text because it finds no other text to speak to in me.'[2]

A friend once described plunging into or out of endeavours as tantrums, unless those shifts were accompanied by real commitment. In my case, moving away from writing was equal parts losing faith, throwing a tantrum and being too early in the navigation of my illness to have known better.

'Have you written lately?' my mom asked, about two years after I had more or less ceased entirely. 'It is a waste of training and talent to let it go, don't you think?'

In an interview, Elizabeth Gilbert talked of the damage that the idea of passion can do to people—convincing them that something is missing if every moment is not 'setting your head on fire'. It was frightening to open my notebook and not be moved to say anything. It was frightening to find language itself alien and inaccessible. The distorting prism of depression made both words and experiences obtuse to me. Gilbert pointed out that in a culture that teaches us 'to fetishize passion above all', moments where we've lost our passion can make us feel 'more excluded and more exiled and, sometimes, like a failure'. She finds that creative endeavours are better served by curiosity than passion.[3]

S sent me submission calls, contest announcements, names of publications to which I should submit work. Even as I was uncertain about re-entering the literary world, her messages allowed me to re-familiarize myself with it. I sent out a tentative submission now and then to literary magazines from the meagre pool of poems I had written. These were mostly met with silence or a 'this isn't quite right for us'. S rarely, if ever, mentioned her wins—big or small. Not necessarily because she wanted to protect me, but possibly because she set less store by them than I did.

She asked me to try and put together a manuscript. I tried. It was a period of trying. With the help of research and therapy, I was beginning to manage my illness differently, recognizing that there were responses and restorative activities that were within my control. I did not want to be helpless. I was taken with the idea of putting together a manuscript. A collection had space for failure, for contradictions—for poems to converse. I was leaving an extended period of stagnation behind and learning. It gave me the impetus to write again.

When I started, the words that emerged were weak, clichéd and rusty. Years later, I encountered a Joshua Jennifer Espinoza poem called 'You Do Not Have to Write the Best Poem in the World'.[4] I struggled, and still struggle, as I suspect many others do, with the idea that one can write without the express purpose of the work being good. Every serious action I performed had to be striving for near perfection, every piece of writing had to not suffer in comparison to someone else's writing.

As someone whose mind is wired to tell me I am awful at everything I attempt, the difficult stage of writing terrible first lines and confused drafts can be incredibly demotivating. One way I learnt to think differently about that process was through Ross Gay's encouragement to writers to strive for mystery rather than mastery.[5] During National Poetry Month[6] in 2015, I tried to write a poem a day in April. I followed, daily, anything that moved me. Something in the day would remind me of an old relationship, and I would try to see where that led; something in the news caught my attention, and I would try to see what it meant to me.

I wrote twenty-two poems in those thirty days at the beginning of this re-entry into writing. S read all of them. I did not need feedback at that moment. I needed a place to send the work—*it is real, I am writing again.* She continued to read hundreds of poems and drafts over the next three years, most of them dreadful. On the rare occasion when she was tired, she would tell me politely she would read the latest after a few days. I was excited by the writing, but unable, still, to tell if it was any good without another person's go-ahead. It was an anxiety-racked process, often wiping me out. But S kept me going.

Even when she got busy as we all do, that initial stability made all the difference—someone to turn me back towards a practice that added to my life, that I was slowly able to figure out how to do again on my own. Sometimes, sustained kindness makes all the difference in one's world. Writing is a part of me—like my relationships, like my therapeutic work. I am not always good at it. I am often frustrated by it. But it is one part of me being a person.

## II

In a classroom in Japan, a student wrote a note to the poet Naomi Shihab Nye, introducing her to the Japanese concept of *yutori*, which loosely translates to 'living with spaciousness'. Yutori, she explained, could refer to everything from the expansion of one's mind that reading a poem enables, to arriving early to a place or an appointment to allow oneself time to look around.[7]

The illness talks constantly—like a roommate who will not shut up, who follows me everywhere. Sometimes, I sit down to write, and I cannot reach the writing voice. There is too much ambient noise; the pathways of the mind are too crowded.

I am blocked. Fatimah Asghar, a poet, points out that 'writer's block' is often dismissed in creative spaces: *There's no such thing.* She argues that that perspective discounts individual experiences of trauma, illness, depression and even everyday mental clutter.[8] Some of us are blocked for systemic, bodily and personal reasons that require taking care of in ways tailored to our particular circumstances and personalities. In the case of my writing, it is a continual see-saw between input and silence that allows it to form. In a field like writing, where the blank page is the farthest point from where I am trying to get to, seeking spaciousness can feel counterintuitive. But when it is loud inside me, when I have a fearful song on loop, there is no room for creative words.

Not only is writing difficult to pursue when I am unwell, trying and failing to write can accentuate the symptoms of mental illness. When weakened by illness, I am more susceptible to spiralling into repetitive, self-denigrating thoughts. *I am unable to say what I want to, I thought this was a decent idea but it is actually terrible and I am an idiot for having seen any potential in it, what a waste of time and energy, other people are writing much smarter things, who am I to take up space by writing, people will hate it and they will be justified in hating it, this is not worth the trouble.*

In the periods when I focus on my health, I pursue empty hours and quiet moments, cultivating space and patience for non-productive, regenerative stillness in my life. I refrain from adding to my task list or my reading list. Spending more time with a single piece of reading becomes a way to wander, to branch out without cluttering the moments of my day. Deliberately spending time away from writing clears the way for its gradual re-emergence—the same way chosen solitude prepares me for being there meaningfully with and for other people.

There is a common perception that creativity and mental illness are linked.[9] The idea endures because of selective takeaways from oft-cited studies, suggesting that creative people are more affected by certain mental illnesses than the general population;[10,11] numerous TV shows, movies and books, featuring tropes of the tortured artist;[12] speculations on a link between pathology and creativity by highly cited ancient thinkers such as Aristotle and Plato;[13] and well-known stories of multiple artists who suffered from, and sometimes died as a result of, mental illness.[14] The proliferation of the idea has given it purchase. But the above studies have been challenged for being highly subjective, and their findings have not been conclusively replicated.[15] The data is further skewed by the difficulty of defining a field as broad and nebulous as creativity, and the fact that people often choose creative professions because they are attracted to them and not necessarily because they are more creative than the general population.

A writer once told me that when she asked a psychiatrist if we stopped being creative if we were cured, if our 'madness' was treated, he told her, 'Yes, if one is treated, one loses the ability to create art.' Besides being a claim with no scientific backing, it is also a dangerous one that potentially discourages people from seeking help. The popular notion that internal chaos aids artistic fodder persists and neglects to consider the severity (and volatility) of symptoms as well as the reality that stability allows for productivity and the pursuit of worthwhile goals.

'The "mad genius" has been a cherished cultural icon for centuries,' writes the American psychologist Judith Schlesinger, 'a romantic and compelling concept that helps demystify our geniuses and make them more accessible. . . . But perhaps the most destructive consequence is when those who truly have serious disorders deny themselves treatment, fearing that it will diminish their gifts (Berlin, 2008; Piirto, 2004), or even "dampen [their] general intellect and limit [their] emotional and perceptual range" (Jamison, 2006a, p. 20).'[16] While not discounting that there are many cases of overlap between those who make art and those with a history of mental illness (I count among them), I have never found therapy, medication and recovery to have hindered my artistic impulses and abilities. Instead, the healthier I am, the clearer and more nuanced the writing is.

I have said before that I did not write in the extremely ill years. When I am in a depressive phase or an anxious spiral, I still do not write, am not capable of writing. I struggled to make peace with these phases till March 2016, when I went to a three-day writing workshop in Bir, Himachal Pradesh. We were invited to a session in the library, where the instructor first asked us to choose any book from the shelves and then, after a brief time perusing it, to read out a passage that spoke to us. The first book I picked up was a collection of poems by Rumi. Opening it at a random page, the following words, from his poem 'Buoyancy', met me,

> Why should we grieve that we have been sleeping?
> It does not matter how long we have been unconscious.
>
> We are groggy, but let the guilt go.
> Feel the motions of tenderness around you, the buoyancy.[17]

Those words have become something of a staple for me, a reminder that grief for the gaps in my productivity, my health and my writing practice are not required of me. The hours spent on other things are forgiven, are in no need of forgiveness. In these periods of rest and relative inactivity, my writing absorbs what Jessica Dore refers to as 'the lushness of the dark'.[18] The dark is charged, is it not, with permission, respite—even promise.

## III

I called X on his birthday, three years and nineteen days after we had split up. We do this—call or text on each other's birthdays, six months apart to my comfort. Outside of these exchanges, ensconced within the safety of familiar ceremonies, we do not sustain a post-break-up friendship. I initiate so few of these conversations that I know we are both alarmed when I ask cautiously if we can talk about something.

I have been sitting with an essay I wrote about our relationship for three months, turning it over in my mind, scribbling minor epiphanies on the bus, sending single sentence emails to myself: *rewrite, but this time without sentiment; rewrite, but this time with empathy.* I am aware that the drafts are missing something—I just cannot pinpoint what in the beginning. It was a story I had been so certain of—choosing to write it early because I needed at that moment a task I knew I would be good at, comfortable in. The story I had told friends, countless times, filled with the minute details of microaggressions and disappearances—that story—I wrote quickly. Easily.

Still, I waited.

'We tell ourselves stories,' Didion wrote, 'in order to live.'[19]

In the wake of a break-up, I told myself stories. I got over him in one week. The entire length of the relationship had been a waste of my time. He had not treated me well. I had only occasionally treated him badly. We tell ourselves stories that sit tidily with our versions of our selves.

In the first months of singledom, I told stories that served my purpose of moving forward. Didion said, 'We try to find the sermon in suicide.' I tried to find the villain in a mismatched equation, the martyr in a see-saw that swung up both ways.

When that purpose had been achieved, the stories shifted. Even the grittiest memories that had once been critical in creating a bulwark between me and returning began to fade. More time had passed since the collapse of the relationship than was spent in it. A story featuring archetypes of long-suffering heroes and villains in need of redemption was no longer good enough on its own. No, I wanted to tell myself a longer, fuller story.

~

I waited, I explained to him, sat with the draft for weeks.

It was frustrating, taking apart the well-worn facts, the carefully and cynically distilled anecdotes to ask myself: What role (if any) had been mine? What besides human error had wrecked this? What does illness require of caregivers?

I tell him I didn't understand him once, not for a long time, but that I did after writing it over and over again till it began to feel like the truest version of the story. Well, the truest version I could achieve at that moment.

I asked him if I could send him the essay. Did he want to read it? There was *no pressure*. I told him that it did not have *that* story or *that* one, that none of this was about grinding an axe, and could he understand what I was saying?

He was annoyed by the mention of *that* story, and I was annoyed by the discomfort seeping into his tone. We ended the call a minute later, having agreed that I would email him and that he would take his time.

~

The truth is I was prepared for the exchange to go badly—it was too late for me to start bartering empathy for connection, understanding for communication. Hadn't I been the one to keep my distance, the one to rebuff every effort to stay friends, the one who thought distancing was an integral part of regaining my mental health? Who did I think I was, laying thousands of words about the past at someone's door, this man I had only known as a boy, whose present circumstances and well-being I knew very little about? Even if he was someone I had spent thousands of words understanding, who I had been astonished and relieved to finally understand. It began to feel like I had crawled out of the blue that I had receded into for years, only to impose on him an emotional burden he hadn't asked for.

He did not call me. He wrote back.

I didn't even read the words the first time—scrolling down, surveying the length of his response before anything else. By the time I had swiped down a few times without reaching the end, I was overwhelmed and put the phone back inside my pocket and cried in the street.

～

The poet Rachel McKibbens wrote, 'Sometimes, we write about it so we don't have to talk about it.'[20]

It was a one-thousand-two-hundred-and-sixty-four-word reply. I could never have said those things to him in person or over the phone, and I doubt he could have said those things back to me. I read it a paragraph at a time. It took me a month to write back, to say thank you—thank you for saying sorry, for the care with which you read it, thank you for not getting angry, for meeting me at that level of uncomfortable depth most people would have run from.

P.S. I remember all the good things. I don't have words for all of them, but I do. I didn't expect you to respond with so much thoughtfulness. It actually stunned me in some way—that we have both become so much more mature than we used to be, that we are having this sincere conversation about our past selves. I was and am really grateful for the way you wrote back.

～

# LOUDER THAN THE MUSIC

*On Family #2*

After spending a couple of years away, I moved home in 2015 on the heels of a job I felt I had failed at, a terminated relationship and worsening mental illness. I was lonely in a preternatural way that had little to do with other people, but I did not know that yet. I conflated community with wholeness, the company of close people with feeling most like myself. I believed my mind would heal if I could rebuild stronger relationships within my family. I thought that if the four of us could repair the roads to one another, we would be set free in a lasting way and the shackles of illness would loosen around me.

Growing up, my family and I would drive from North Goa to South Goa on the weekends. On the flat road between Porvorim and Utorda, where the rain trees on either side of the road meet to form a dappled shade, the cassette player (later, a CD player) played REM, Tracy Chapman, America, Billy Joel, Don McLean.

Sometimes, I would be the first to sing along, followed by another voice—a supplementary singing arising in response to my own. Or I would be the one that followed, easy as. We would sing deeper into our voices when we hit the chorus of a song—making the song more real than it was the moment before.

⁓

In my family, sometimes, it is easy. We hand over and accept what is needed willingly. We feel generous—both the givers and recipients of loyalty. Other times, we are scarce in our sense of fealty. We snap in the wake of one more ask placed upon us, one more denied or resisted expectation. The details do not matter. What matters is that the breakage—which we have inflicted upon each other—has rendered us both brittle and strong. We swing between the two states in relation to one another—operating from rooms deep inside ourselves with vantage points only we can see, channels battened down from the outside, misunderstanding one another, seeing things differently no matter how many times we've listened to each other's perspective. We ride this carousel of conflict and reprieve, this carousel of playing the aggressor and the aggrieved.

Each of us has our own story, a complex system of threads that leads back from our mistakes to the highly specific reasons for our layered personalities. We return to the fold, tired, a little jaded, to talk ourselves back to one another, to attempt empathy, to put envy, resentment, insecurity to the test, releasing it into our shared world in a controlled, careful environment. These conversations are watching our stories in reverse—a hurt wound back to a source. To be able to talk is a gift. Though we may be differently endowed with the necessary openness, there are ethereally calm moments when even the most closely guarded member's story trickles out—miraculously and in their own words.

A friend posted saying, '[A] strong, thriving relationship with one's parents can result in unfathomable peace, and in turn provide healing. It takes time, effort and tears, but ah—it is worth it.' Imagining such a peace, such an existence, requires a faith I do not always have. I lean into the moments when I do. Another friend tells me to put my trust in time—it makes family softer.

When I hear people describe certain families as toxic, I wonder if there is something more rewarding than outright rejection or complete acceptance. I recognize that I do not need to continue to pursue the fostering and healing of these relationships; that there are valuable lives to be lived outside of these systems.

What are the choices open to me when it comes to family? Return. Stillness. Movement. In her poem, 'Dear P.', Victoria Chang writes, 'when I ask the tree which / way it just points in every direction.'[1] I have not yet been able to remain of one mind about what it means to be family. All the time, there are signs I should remain interspersed with rubble, clues about missing epiphanies mixed in with half-hearted impulses to bolt.

Yet, I fray more away from home.

I am amused at my friend who cries on two- or three-day trips because she misses her family. I cannot understand why my family cries as my cousin departs after her wedding. Yet, deep within, I know I am the one who does not leave. I am the one who knows the honest answer to the question, 'Where are you from?' *I am from them.*

∼

I have pored intensely over some problems in therapy—how to cope, how to distance myself from the anxiety within me, how to develop a voice and a will that can resist the depression, how to be a multitude of selves because a single self cannot hold my straining ill mind. It is too dangerous, too limiting to remain one self for too long.

Nayantara, the Mumbai therapist I spoke to on and off for three years, focused on the present, the week gone by. It was the most useful approach at a time in my life when regaining a modicum of control over my ability to do basic tasks (wake up, eat healthily, get through the workday) was my one urgent goal. After I moved away from Mumbai, I continued to speak to her through video calls and over the phone.

She was funny. She stayed engaged during our conversations—gently pushing back against my closely held but little-examined ideas. She laughed—the most genuine, full-throated, endearing laughter—when we came upon a particularly ridiculous realization. She was the first professional that helped me understand and manage my illness. When I see a stranger who looks like her on the street or wears her smile, I am still momentarily disarmed.

When I first started therapy, a friend of mine, P, asked me with concern if I was paying someone to be my friend. P did not ask unkindly—she was right in that I needed someone in my corner. But my therapist was not a friend; she was the other side of the chessboard. She outmanoeuvred the compelling and twisted pathways of my mind—unknotting the confusion I was mired in to reach a clearing over and over again.

The world of recovery I had built was missing key pieces. The time I had spent working on my illness and the depth

I had ascribed to my therapy sessions helped obscure what I had neglected to address. A particularly severe mental health relapse brought this fact into unavoidable focus—illness aside, I was not at peace.

~

Against instincts warning me to not pry open that can of worms, I once narrate a story about family to Nayantara. *They . . . I . . . Back then . . . We drove back in silence.* She was quiet. She said, 'That is emotional abuse.' I shut her down immediately. We had started to move from story to implication, moral, consequence. Not every move is rational. I only knew that I had to stamp out the spark before it became a flame.

After that time, I was amazed that she still believed I had any capacity for self-awareness at all. We never spoke of it again. If she had asked—she sometimes checks where I am with a problem I had brought up in a previous session—I would have said, 'Oh, that? That doesn't feel like a priority right now.'

After I told her, I wanted to obliterate the memory, to never have told her. If I could not make her forget, I wanted her to perform the same time-warping and pain-blunting exercise I have performed a million times: *We are all different people now. Only I remember this. Memory is suggestible. They were acting out of what they knew at the time. My experience is not very different from many of the people I grew up around. It was a '90s thing.*

I used to call her my bullshit filter. We both used to laugh at this. We were both proud of how willing I seemed to be to look behind the curtain. I was not afraid of confronting how complicated I can be, how little of a monolith. But I shut her down that time because some things do not feel like they are safe to acknowledge, especially not to another person.

I did not continue with her for too many sessions after that.

⌒

I am sitting—as I suspect most of us are—on a mountain of accumulated memories. I can run a thread back through them when I pause to wonder why a single, stray remark at the dinner table can unnerve me so. When an old wound is awakened, I have no centre. What am I afraid of? I cannot say—only that a wildness stirs, a primitive instinct for aggressive self-preservation emerges. I am a child, a teenager, an adult, all in the same moment, and I collapse into anger. Sometimes, I can trace the implosion cleanly back to a source, *they said I—, they did—*. Sometimes, I can only call it dread and be unable to dissect it further. I feel embarrassment and despair when I see that despite years of therapy, I can still be reduced to anxious fury by the faintest whiff of danger. Sometimes, I imagine the dragon into the room. Combat is what I sense, and combat is what I respond to—springing the conflict into existence. Other times, I do not start it, but I do not walk away—helping spur the fire into an inferno.

⌒

The bouts of depression and anxiety were deepened by the unresolved webs within me. The illness and the wrought equations with my family adversely affected one another. When this occurred, there was no centre to fall back on, no stable sense of self. I turned to a person in my life that had made peace with difficult demons. She was middle-aged and had survived trauma. She credited a particular therapist with helping her get there. What drew me to her story was that she had learnt how not to be destabilized by other people's behaviour—a skill that has always eluded me.

There is therapy that is affirming and heartening, that makes me laugh and weaves lightness into my day. Then, there is the kind that transacts in discomfort, which takes time and invariably has a cost. I came away from the early sessions with the new therapist, Sonali, feeling uneasy. Therapy was not *supposed* to disturb elements inside me.

A few weeks after our sessions began, there was a family conflict I walked away from calmly, because some part of my mind had decided to commit to the work of changing lifelong patterns. The rest of me was tired and coming apart. There were more loose parts inside me than before. I was not succeeding at the simple task of being consistently mature. What was the point of the excruciating work I was doing in therapy—revisiting memories and examining my enabling and harmful roles—if I was not making adequate progress?

It was the hardest thing I had ever tried to work through—the most recursive, the one that most often made me feel foolish. I was yelling at myself to get over it already even as I went to therapy and tried to work on it. The process of learning to retrain my instincts was difficult. There are so many plateaus on the path to recovery—and when I am in them, they appear to run ceaselessly into the distance in front of me.

My therapist and I circled in a sort of stalemate, as I raged against why I could not *help myself*, why my temper raged like a child's. We worked, exhaustingly, on conflicts that belonged to a handful of templates that repeated themselves. She had me record events that troubled me, asked me to retell stories till I was not skimming over any part, till I was tired of the telling, of rehashing the prosaic and the humiliating.

It was tedious work. I noted down flaws in my well-worn logic—creating flow charts and listing where a train of thought broke down, and why, along with possible explanations for the reason I had made missteps and how I might course-correct. This process became a way to map and understand myself, not just inside my mind, but on paper, with an audience and a record—with someone who was neither a loved one nor an enemy, someone trained in the architecture of the mind.

I hated having to explain myself. It was suffocating to circle the stale cauldron of a single story. But I saw how a narrative changes when I am forced to explain each bit, I saw how it gets clearer, how the chinks stick out, how it leaves breathing room for my roles and reactions to reveal themselves, and how it creates opportunities to move forward.

I see how I have caused myself grief by ascribing a contrived logic to others' love. I tell my therapist that I hate that my family needs me so much. 'What do they need you for?' she asks, prodding me to be specific. I rattle off a list of tasks for which they depend on me. She tries to unravel each of my disjointed threads back to one source or the other, and I resist her. I want the threads to stay together, banded together in confusion and complexity. When she separates them, they travel down a path that leads to an answer so obvious that I am angry to be have been led there. The untangling suggests their perceived need for me serves a purpose for me too. Perhaps I feel that their need for me qualifies my inclusion in their ranks. She points to the members of my family who do not contribute as much. 'Has anyone abandoned them?' she asks. Sometimes, therapy makes me feel like an adolescent frozen in time.

I saw a father and son step out of a car recently. The son waited by the back while his father unloaded grocery bags and handed them to him quietly. I was confused. This was not my understanding of family. I would have done it differently. I would have started yelling before the car had even stopped that everyone needed to help me; I wouldn't have even considered that someone could wait patiently, wordlessly for their share of a simple chore. I would not have considered that I had a choice between yelling and hauling the bags myself. Being nice would mean asking politely, would mean squelching the sense inside me that I should not have to ask at all. The man and his son and their grocery bags unnerved me.

With time, I have become less opaque to myself. There is a slow science to extracting the parts of me still lodged in the past. I could not resist pushing people to morph into what I considered better, healthier versions of themselves. Most of the time, this caused them to lose their patience with me, their composure. I caused explosions—sometimes tiny, sometimes spectacular—because any reaction was better than no reaction when I could not sit still with my emotions.

There are moments in limited-overs cricket when the fielder gives up the chase, when he knows that the ball will find the boundary long before he gets to it. I watch with reverence as a man slows down, comes to a halt in surrender to what has revealed itself to be inevitable. Maybe there is not a lesson in everything. But watching the man surrender, I am drawn to his intelligence, to his careful conservation of energy. There is a point—and he recognizes it—where his body cannot be pushed further, cannot give that little bit extra except in vain. Increasingly, this feels like a story that requires the right kind of surrender.

Increasingly, I have come to treat difficult situations with a growing degree of healthy detachment, instead of walking back into them as if I have no agency, as if every evoked emotion demands a requisite action. But the changes are so gradual and so small, no one else in my family can honestly say they have noticed them. 'Have I not changed?' I ask, still seeking someone else's validation. The fact that they have not noticed causes its own kind of anxiety: Was I kidding myself? I am learning to trust that I have changed apropos of nothing except my judgement.

I bump every day into the temptation to be drawn back into conflict. It is what I am used to. It is, in a twisted way, what I am good at. I know the moves, I know the disappointment that awaits me, and I walk towards it anyway. The smallest ember, an incendiary remark relayed second-hand, can spur me into the volatile state right before reaction. It is not linear or easy, and the work is far from over.

~

'People do not change, not really,' my mother tries to drill into me. I see the truth in her words around me—my sister still struggles with balance, my father is still saying the wrong words, she is still learning to apologize and I am still hoping each of us will change into who I wish us to be.

But time is odd—humbling. I see how balance has a place in my sister's life now, I see how her choosing herself has become a good thing. I see how my parents use a more expansive vocabulary for pain. I see how our moving forward is tempered by stagnation and regression. I see how strong, even if warped, the love is. That has been my progress: to acknowledge that I do not leave because I am loved.

In the six years since my grandmother has passed, each year has brought new awareness of the conversations I could have with her now that I couldn't before. *When did you start writing? What did it mean to you? Did you write a story about the Valley of Flowers? I remember it, but I can't find it anywhere.* I want so much more from her now than I did when I was younger. Time has not been a guarantee for change in my family, and certainly not a guarantee for growth. But it has pulled from me realizations I could never have imagined, that I could never have arrived at without the aiding passage of time. One of the most humbling of those revelations has been that I had more common ground with my grandmother than I imagined—it was the limits of what I knew that hid from me that I would one day want to hear her tell me stories again, that I would one day regret having been so very young and rigid while she was alive.

⌒

Some change in our equations has been organic—like me and my sister getting closer while fundamentally disagreeing on a litany of things. When I am upset, she plays a game of Scrabble with me. It is one of the mind's greatest kindnesses that a game can tame its turmoil, can put its energies to enjoyable use at a moment when that does not seem possible. It is one of this relationship's greatest gifts that we have chosen, after many missteps, to play without points, to gamely appreciate each other's good words, to play till the tiles run out.

I explained to a friend that I get along better with my sibling when we both hold our tongues—what we do not say being as important as what we do say. It can feel like a lie, a dishonest compromise. He felt the same way with his sibling. It is easy to slip into thoughts of '*this isn't a real family, these relationships feel fake and hollow*'. Perhaps we will never enjoy a cosmic closeness or stay in touch when we are not living in the same house. Perhaps she will continue to turn down my offers to teach her a recipe, a skill. What she needs is not what I have needed in the past. I may never quite master the art of not saying things that alienate her.

We don't agree on what one should be afraid of—home invasions and compromised privacy or appearing rude to the other's friends, adopting our parents' worst qualities or not being able to match their good ones. We never ship the same couples on a TV show. Sometimes, I think the songs she listens to sound like static forced through musical organs. Always, she finds annoying my habit of listening to my current favourite song on loop. We are so different that we are always rooting for different sorts of transgressions.

But, over time, I have seen something in the newly open space where one does not say the things that one knows the other person is not willing to receive. There is a version of myself that only comes out here—goofy, unarmed, stupid. She is amazed by the volume at which I sing along to music at home. 'How,' she asks in exasperation, 'can you be louder than the music?'

When I am able to be that unrestrained around her, how can I not?

~

Like loneliness, discomfort must be made a home of. Discomfort with hard truths, jagged edges. With time, with effort, we have each moved forward in some way—less worry; less interference; more tact, which is a different, kinder strain of honesty. We take the moments we get. We retreat when we cannot align. When inevitably our ends arrive, I hope we will have moved further towards one another—if not in closeness, then in understanding. On a molecular level, I want to continue to approach a state between fragile and hardened, at once malleable and muscular in the face of love that is both difficult and tensile.

~

# WHAT IS NEXT IS WHAT THE STORY MOST REQUIRES[1]

*On Suicide*

The dream goes like this—I am driving at night on a route with almost no turns, no cars that I can remember. Only the car's light hitting a length of tar. I reach the jetty at the coast's edge. I haven't visited this site in years, still, the dream doesn't lack detailing. Steps serpentine upwards to a viewpoint that looks out to laterite rocks and a wide, dark sea. The enclosure is empty—presumably because it is night. I have only ever seen it peopled, pulsing—but the place has been erased to silence, a solitude with no bystanders.

I have this dream despite a literature class in high school where the teacher informed us that drowning wasn't gentle, despite the fact that I love the swaddling quality of water, despite the dream's refusal to show me what happens beyond the railings.

Can bodies be recovered from the open ocean? I have little idea, and I know better than to move towards the answer. There is no step small enough in that direction to be innocuous.

The dream also goes like this—I am in possession of a gun. I am in the apartment I have lived in, on and off, for ten years. I do move forward in this one. It is loud and messy. This particular dream doesn't visit me very often.

The dream goes a third way. I have to explain myself. *It was an accident.*

The average cost of suicide is six other people. I calculate three or four in my case. If I include those that I assume will be hurt but will transcend the pain, it is a much larger sampling of people. In the third dream, only the first group is allowed to hold me accountable. Every time, I say by way of explanation, 'It was an accident.'

An artist named Ralph Barton opened the seminal medical textbook, *Grey's Anatomy*, to a page with a diagram of the human heart and shot himself.[2] What people choose to leave behind can be opaque.

After a loved one was rescued from one of her attempts, we went about like puzzle-makers piecing together her night. Shortly before the attempt, she had sent the complete text of Dylan Thomas's poem 'Do Not Go Gentle into That Good Night' to a friend. Because she has never explained any of her attempts—and we suspect she's blocked some of that time out—I have never asked her why she sent a poem about not going quietly when forced to.

> Though wise men at their end know dark is right . . .
> They do not go gentle into that good night.[3]

Her blood-alcohol level was so high that we don't know if an explanation even exists in some recess of her mind. What we know is that the right to answers is not a guaranteed one, no matter the range of one's suffering. I'll admit that mixed with worry and sadness is revulsion and fury—a spool of kerosene swirling in what I thought till that moment was a clear pool of love.

As we leave the hospital, we run into the surgeon who was on call when she was brought into the ER. Impatient with her desire to end her life when he worked daily to save them, he says to her by way of medical advice, 'Don't ever be so stupid again.' We're all quiet with hurt and protective indignation.

But in the following days—in the wake of her silence, in the glaring lack of an apology (yes, at the time we thought we were owed one)—anger rises periodically that sounds a lot like the doctor's: jagged, running on fumes with little room for sympathy.

What people leave behind outside of *the final hours* becomes of monumental significance to the ones who loved them. Books, journals, a life's worth of decisions on friendships, marriage, sacrifice, children, real estate, what they chose to constitute in that life. Where can these maps possibly and meaningfully lead those left behind? In working backwards through a person's life for clues, each piece of information gains vital importance, and every version of the answer invariably comes up short.

~

I often spend time in a place I am going to call *The Brink*. The Brink is not a productive place. It isn't some training ground to understand *what is really important in life*. The Brink is a variant of rock bottom, which doesn't require anything to be externally wrong. It is just somewhere I find myself from time to time. The logic of The Brink is simple—take a good thing in my life and chew on it till it lacks any redemption in my eyes, take an opportunity I have been given and see it is as a pressure and a burden, take objectively difficult things from my life and roll around in them like a kid in sand. Sometimes, I can tell why I'm there. Months of physical pain from injuries. A difficult relationship. Medication withdrawal. But learning *why* is not an exercise that yields any insight on how to leave. Now, The Brink is depression on steroids. It is a volatile place imbued with fury and despair—and those two things in combination suggest violence. I am violently angry at people. I don't mean physical violence, but emotional volatility that impacts and destabilizes others. The language and meaning available in The Brink are whittled down to the basics. The Brink is where I say to myself: *I am done, I quit, I have been given more than I can handle, everyone sucks, but I suck more, thank you but no thank you, life.*

When I am there, I think about the phrase 'quality of life' a lot. Towards the end of her life, my grandmother couldn't take it any more. She would cut out articles about euthanasia from the newspaper, store them in a file and hand them to me. After a while, I stopped reading what she handed to me. When she died, it was of natural causes. I found a letter from her a couple of years after her death in a book of Hindi poems she had gifted me, which I hadn't cracked opened until then. It was illegible because the Parkinson's tremors were at their most advanced stage by then. I wonder what a person restricted to their room, who ventures out occasionally into the corridor with the assistance of a walker, writes about to her granddaughter, who isn't particularly patient. Is it one more *set me free* letter, one last set of instructions: *How to live a life that is deeply unpleasant and that people won't let you quit.*

I sorted through her papers four years after her death because I was moving to a new house and couldn't put it off any longer. She'd signed over the royalties of her books to me before the illness progressed and writing became impossible. I took that to mean that these leftover papers and books were mine to keep. I found Hindi school essays of mine, photographs of one of her book launches, daily household accounts in a calendar diary in a shaky scrawl—Bread (10 rupees), Kit Kat (10 rupees). The mention of Kit Kat levelled me. Every page felt like untenable guilt. *This woman tried to hold me close. This woman was my family, and I did little to nothing to stem her loneliness.*

I couldn't stand how depressed she was, so I avoided her. Even back then, I was afraid it was a condition that was contagious.

What quality of life do chronically depressed people have? At the best of times, experiences are a little bit blunted, a little bit blurred for me. Even when I'm well or stable, I feel a pervasive reluctance to participate in life. It manifests as a desire, ranging from mild to intense, to draw the curtains and stay in bed. The architecture of my days is erratic, without accurate tools to predict how low I will feel when I wake up. If I closely monitor the consumption of daily comforts such as coffee and tea, the regularity of exercise and exposure to sunlight, medication, therapy, screen time, fresh air in a polluted city, and the balance between work and rest, between social interaction and rest—I generally cope. An extraordinary amount of work keeps my illness in check, but no amount of effort can make it disappear.

Sometimes I feel it building—a low-grade panic moving inwards and outwards, growing incrementally as I watch a game or meet a friend or fetch a drink of water. It finally settles into a weight. I recognize it, which is the solution and the problem. I know it will pass, and I know it will return.

When I have arrived at The Brink, I despair about the quality of life I can expect to have. Is this what my days will resemble from here on out? It is a dangerous descent in thought, because at that moment I believe that my reasoning makes perfect sense. It is dangerous because in the midst of that tumult, I believe that the tumult is the sum of my existence. On these terrifying days, I beg God (close to the precipice, belief arrives) and the body for the respite of sleep so that a little rest may sit between me and the non-stop clamour, between me and the pressing need to reaffirm or disavow a will to continue. When I'm better, I tell myself over and over: *Try to remember, not every line of thinking deserves to be honoured. I have more than one set of instincts inside me; trust the one telling me to live.*

~

Jennifer Michael Hecht wrote a compendium of arguments against suicide called *Stay*—reasons ancient and new from philosophy, religion, science. She cautioned that 'there are people reading this who do not see themselves as at risk for suicide but who will die that way, unless they take some mental action now.'[4] Gregory Howe Colt, a writer who spent eight years researching suicides, wrote, '[T]he barriers our culture erects between "normal" people and "suicidal" people [are] barriers that I believe we erect from the fear that the difference is so slight.'[5]

For the longest time, I didn't consider myself one of *those people*—the ones at risk of suicide, even though major depressive disorder is one of the most common root causes. I know my friends and family don't see me as at-risk either. Instead, I fell into the habit of telling people casually that I was not *that kind* of person, that I would never do that to my parents. I visit hospitals more or less regularly, I show up for therapy, I talk to people, I diligently read up on my illness, and I evolve when a particular coping mechanism proves to be inadequate or crashes and burns—*people as careful as me* can always walk themselves back from The Brink.

But because I studied Shakespeare, I know the appearance of a raven in a play spells doom. And because I watch a lot of television, I know that when a character professes that they will not go down a certain path or if it is suggested a character has a long life ahead of them, it is a set-up, a hint that a backflip of circumstances is on the cards, that the opposite may come to pass.

None of the people who I reassure that I will live have ever asked me or looked to me for reassurance that I will stay alive. I have been walking around telling my loved ones for reasons that have nothing to do with those people. I tell myself that

I wouldn't do that to the following list of people—X, Y, Z—
running through the list as a reminder that the last of that
list would have to be dead for me to even *consider* it. But
I'm foreshadowing a possibility I won't admit to myself. So
recently, I have started admitting to myself that I'm part of
a large at-risk population, because when I sink, I can sink
subterraneanly low.

~

'We know a mastodonic amount about suicide,' wrote the
clinical psychologist Kay Redfield Jamison.[6] The mastodon
was an elephantine animal of a size no one living has ever
seen. The bones alone, pulled from the earth around North
America, weigh between seven and eleven thousand kilograms.
The people who have summarized our understanding of
suicide as scientists, sociologists and philosophers on the
subject agree that our collective knowledge runs staggeringly
deep. Imagine the mastodon as a solid structure—for
example, a piggy bank. Break the mastodon open, and out
pour coins—each one bearing a fact or finding about suicide.
But deep as that river runs, another researcher on suicide,
Karl Menninger, admitted, 'It is a durn mystery, you know,
in spite of all we've written about it.'[7]

When Jamison, who suffers from bipolar disorder
and who survived a suicide attempt in her twenties, set
out to write a contemporary bible on suicide, she saw the
undertaking as an avenue towards self-preservation. She
said, 'As a tiger tamer learns the moods and moves of his
cats, and a pilot about the dynamics of the wind and air,

I learnt about the illness I had and its possible endpoint. I learnt as best I could, and as much as I could, about the moods of death.'[8]

~

In a poem about her father standing on a bridge long before she was conceived and contemplating a final leap into the water, Chanda Feldman wrote, 'You will never know the future, so you can bear to go forward.'[9] At the very least, the future includes for most people some of the following—a miscarriage; some kind of assault or illness; losing a job; being left at the start, middle or close to the end in ways that shatter them; discrimination; an iteration of the words 'you should sit down for this', two or three complete overhauls of one's life; being saddled with a shitty in-law or a shitty relative; legal troubles; a call that needs answering in the middle of the night; making desperate calls of one's own to numbers that stay just outside of searchlights.

The future is a nifty place for holding hope. When I was unhappy as a child, all I had to do was tell myself that adulthood was a means to extract myself from this life and propel myself into a life whose interiors would be fitted out to my specifications with a cinematic level of difficulty and bad luck. Whichever era was next felt more solid, less unreliable. When I was first depressed, I was convinced marriage and a dog would fix it. I had this image of returning to an apartment bathed in yellow light—in Mumbai, where I then worked—to a spouse and a dog. The future remained useful in the art of going forward.

I didn't know the future, so I could bear to keep going. Do we continue to live because we cannot be forewarned of life's myriad tragedies and pains? Losing a job, a marriage, lawsuits, a sick child or sibling or partner. If I could have seen in 2012 what the six years beyond held, I would have been devastated. The last few years have dismantled every illusion, every familiar construct for a life. But because I have encountered that future a bit at a time, not all at once as a very overwhelmed and naive twenty-year-old, I have learnt to fashion a different kind of existence than the one I had imagined.

$\sim$

After an experience of cancer, Arthur W. Frank set about trying to understand the role of storytelling in the circle of illness and health. He describes writing *The Wounded Storyteller* in similar terms to Jamison when he says it was 'as much a work of healing as of scholarship'.[10] He suggested that the stories of the ill and the wounded fit into three broad narrative types.

He saw the Restitution Narrative as a utopian story adopted by the patient who believes that recovery is imminent and absolute, that time can be wound backwards by the miracles of modern medicine to a moment of perfect health. It is a narrative that leans on the idea that one's health has only been misplaced, and once found, one's life can resume its former course. It is a line of storytelling that leads to unfathomable heartbreak for the patient—who must learn that recovery can be non-linear, tenuous, incomplete and even temporary.

On the other hand, those people who succumb to the Chaos Narrative view their illness as a labyrinth without an exit. The storyteller of chaos doesn't comprehend how one moment morphs into another and crumbles under the changes and challenges of a new and unpredictable existence.

The Quest Narrative, the one Frank believes facilitates recovery, is the storytelling of resilience. It is a story that accepts illness and sets out to carve a new life from and around it. As Lucille Clifton writes:

> I made it up,
> here on this bridge between
> starshine and clay,
> my one hand holding tight
> my other hand . . .

Frank saw that most ill people choose all three kinds of stories at different moments in their illness, sometimes alternately between chaos and quest, sometimes between restitution and chaos.

It is a shifting pattern of storytelling that I recognize within myself. I am elated when I have good days, despair when I get worse again. In each truly bad episode, I am convinced that my life will be nothing but a series of dips descending unexpectedly and frequently. I send a friend a text containing the words: *Each time I have another prolonged depressive episode, my tolerance wears a little thinner.* It is the stories we tell ourselves that we are most convinced by.

At my worst can't-get-out-of-bed or open-the-curtains moments, what my illness verbalizes feels louder, clearer and more consistent than the other parts of myself. After all, the illness is pinning me to my mattress, and the rest of me is a feeble protestor easily overridden by the illness. I succumb to my Chaos Narrative at times. Other times, I am enamoured by the possibility of a Restitution Narrative—one that will allow me to be *limitless.*

The early years of being sick were dominated by this stubborn understanding and toxic hope that I could be *fixed, cured.* Someone could fix it, a marriage, a new doctor, a new medicine, an exercise routine, an endless stream of crafting projects. The vocabulary of coping and managing reached me later. It takes time for a condition to reveal itself as transitory, semi-permanent or chronic. Some people experience mental illness as a season from which they eventually emerge.

It took me five years—of falsely interpreting every good phase as a sign that I was permanently *cured*—to accept that my disorders were, for the time being, chronic. No one relationship (however loving) and no one practice (however fulfilling) would fix this. There were limits to what a long-term therapist could teach me. No matter how much work was behind me, there is more ahead because I *am* ill.

*Present continuous tense.*

When I ceased to expect travelling back in time, I found a bewildering, unexpected life that I hadn't imagined was possible. I had stayed the course of suffering by trying to turn back. In the present, I found a profound, if turbulent, joy in writing, friendship, love, even myself. I continue to struggle with the contradictions of recovery, but I can better ride the sine wave between the highs and the *low* lows. I learnt that in my journey, the mastery of my illness wasn't mastery over symptoms so much as one over misguided expectations.

~

I spent a long time believing that we have the choice to terminate our lives at a moment of our choosing, that certain people were going to embrace that choice no matter what. I hadn't been able to see a future for myself stretch out beyond those first bleak and incomprehensible years of illness. But as I crossed birthdays (twenty-three, twenty-four . . .) that I hadn't expected to reach, I kept thinking: *I'm alive. I made it to a once-distant destination.* When I celebrated ten years of a close friendship with a hike—*Alive.* When the first baby in my friend circle was born—*Alive.*

I had arrived at a future I had stopped envisioning, stopped noticing.

On the handful of nights when I really, truly considered it, I would reach out to friends. One said to me, 'Mornings are wiser than evenings,' and I went to sleep. Another said, 'It will be FINE,' in angry, concerned capital letters, and spoke to me for many hours till I was convinced that there was a chance I could be F-I-N-E. I found myself always a tiny bit grateful and astonished to wake up the next morning, a little less destroyed than the night before. Surviving difficult times, as Hecht once described, becomes a sowing and a kind of reaping—'Every day must be borne, and the reward for bearing it is another day.'[11]

The periods I spend in that dark realm between determination and hopelessness have gradually shrunk as I learnt the feelings are finite—if not vanquishable, then controllable. And that I could have moments of happiness before and after devastating sadness.

What encourages people to decide that they or their lives aren't worth it? The longer I survived and the more I read, I saw that my allegiance to choice originated from generalized ideas about freedom and choice as inalienable and universal, without a thoughtful weighing of where our individual and collective ideas of freedom emerge from. Hecht argued that people 'make life and meaning together, in the context of others', and if 'society is in any way complicit in making us hate ourselves', we shouldn't 'listen to it invite the miserable to die and get out of the way'.[12]

When people die because of their illness, the illness leads one to the precipice and powers the act. I do not believe it is a crime, but it is a tragedy for people to suffer, to arrive at hopelessness and to die because of their mental illnesses.

~

In the wake of a high-profile suicide, there is an outpouring of opinions and emotional responses—some from those whose lives have been touched by attempts or completions, and some who have experienced it in a second-, third- or fourth-hand way, perhaps simply from the news or the grapevine. Some of the responses boil down to—*No, why, my heart is breaking, come back, the world isn't better without yo*u. Some of it isn't interested in the why and is more aggressive—*How could you, this isn't fair.*

The outpouring can be as confusing for people with mental illness as the actual death. People who would never think to check on their mentally ill friends on days when a celebrity suicide hits the news will post the earth-shattering words, *You are not alone, we are here.* It is an intra-planetary rescue team signing up to respond to distress signals—a service that there is presently little evidence to believe they will deliver.

Anne Lamott, who's been writing about the purpose of hope and community for a long time, wrote, 'Ram Dass . . . said that ultimately we're all just walking each other home. I love that. I try to live by it.'[13]

When not confronted with the crisis of death, we often forget that we're all just walking each other home.

～

We're taught, ad nauseam, that we are capable of infinite strength. Brene Brown, maverick of the bravery and vulnerability age, said humans are 'wired for struggle'.[14] Her assertion bears out when I look at people who have surmounted circumstances greater than mine. A woman who lost her fiancé in a freak accident, and countless others who have survived and continue to navigate caste, class and religious discrimination. And yet, my despair isn't squashable, isn't some luxury I have chosen to buy into. Every time I fall ill again, I think of all the people who suggest mentally ill people should get better after a course of therapy and medication, who believe that simple relationships exist between cause and effect, between the degree of effort and quality and durability of the outcome.

The threshold for suicide is lower in people with mental illness. What does strength mean in that circumstance? The amount of time a person has endured is both an indication of the length of the suffering and the amount of time they have succeeded in persisting. If facts are a ledge to hold on to, studies find that, overwhelmingly, people who are rescued after attempts go on to live full lives. They express explicit relief at being saved. It is important to acknowledge that this isn't a uniform phenomenon; some people go on to make further attempts—some of whom die by it. Of the 515 people who were rescued from the Golden Gate Bridge over thirty-five years, only thirty-five were found by Richard Seiden to have died later by suicide.[15] An overview of 177 studies around the world (with the exclusion of Africa) revealed that only an average of 4.2 per cent of people who had been rescued would die by suicide in the following ten years. Over a longer follow-up period, there is a gradual increase. A thirty-seven-year study of 100 survivors found that 13 per cent had died by suicide in that period. But 87 per cent were alive or had died from different causes.[16]

~

Hope doesn't have to be a meaningless abstraction. It can be a radical engine geared to propel a life to a different moment in time. The poet Jeff Hardin wrote:

Still, I have a faith that what is next is what
the story most requires so that the shape
of time allotted, ordained to be, can then
reveal itself.[17]

One of my friends hesitates before she tells me, 'If you had told me in college that you had a mood disorder or that you were depressed . . . I would have chalked it up to your lack of religious life.' When we talk about suicide, she says she sometimes believes it happens less to people who pray. She explains, 'I know it is not that simple. It is not that you won't have issues, but that there is real, actual strength that comes from God. So prayer is complex. It is not about praying twenty sentences before bed or these many visits to church or anything like that. It is about a relationship that makes living possible—amazing—full of hope and joy.'

I don't share my friend's faith or her reasoning, but I find that within reason, the tenets of faith resemble the tenets of radical reimagining and survival. The living that is possible for my friend through God is also possible through other kinds of faith, the faith that your community or your art or your sheer determination to draw water from stone will carry you into a place where you can endure.

Gregory Boyle is a priest in Los Angeles who works to support and rehabilitate former and current gang members. He speaks of vastness, greatness—the expansive and elastic spiritual space he believes is available to each of us. He pushes people to see that no matter how large they perceive experience and possibility to be, it is larger still with a view that rolls out for miles and miles ahead of us. He sees existence as an entity, whose limits can be pushed from inside the contours of our minds.[18]

In becoming the opposite of who I thought I was—open, sentimental—it is malleability that has seen me through. All of the emotions and experiences I thought I was past when I fell sick, I circle again. I swing down each of those roads again, and I have to unlearn conviction, rigidity. I have to be open to the idea that I will continue to encounter more than I believed existed.

Why we endure or succumb is as unknowable as why we fall sick in the first place. In a letter to Cheryl Strayed's advice column, 'Dear Sugar', a reader asked, 'What the fuck, what the fuck, what the fuck? I'm asking this question as it applies to everything every day.' Strayed wrote a lengthy answer revisiting sexual abuse in her childhood and said it took her years to internalize the understanding that 'some things are so sad and wrong and unknowable that the question must simply stand alone like a spear in the mud'. She ended her letter by telling the reader to 'ask better questions' of his life.[19]

I have moved slowly and reluctantly, non-linearly and begrudgingly from asking *why I am depressed, why I can't be cured, I have put in my time, Goddammit, can I really take more days and weeks like this* to *what can I do, what makes this liveable, what allows for the fullest and most forgiving life.*

# WAITING FOR SUNBIRDS

*On the Natural World*
*As a Space for Healing*

[T]here are, on this planet alone, something like two
million naturally occurring sweet things,
some with names so generous as to kick
the steel from my knees: agave, persimmon,
stick ball, the purple okra I bought for two bucks
at the market.

—Ross Gay, 'Sorrow Is Not My Name'[1]


During the weekly hour of therapy, I am restless, twitchy.
I want to keep my attention within my therapist's well-lit
room, small and covered in paintings. So while we speak, I
am always drawing—a diversionary activity that utilizes my
nervous energy and frees up my mind. She doesn't protest
that only occasionally do I look her in the eye, that regardless
of whether I am the one speaking or she is, I keep furiously
running oil pastels over the page.

A few times during the therapy hour, I switch to a pen
and scribble a note I would benefit from remembering,
reinforcing, internalizing: *Transition from old patterns, grow
my peace* . . . At the end, she usually asks what I have been
drawing. It is always botanical: elementary branches, shrubs,
pots, flowers curved around the notes. Sometimes, it is only

a colour palette: earthy tones turned into an orb or blended into slats. I have worked her green, brown and yellow pastel crayons down to nubs.

To repair, to cope, I have had to rely on more than the purely verbal. I have developed a painting habit for when I know my mind needs a break: I follow simple YouTube tutorials on how to paint crabs, robins, wisteria flowers—it is freeing to follow the step-by-step instructions. When a verbal one seems inadequate, I turn to this visual language. The wildlife biologist Alan Rabinowitz, who grew up with a stutter, became interested in non-verbal communication when he realized he was able to communicate with animals. Outside of, or in combination with, words, there are legitimate pathways to shape meaning, build peace and forge connection (especially with myself).

When I reopen the drawings and notes from my therapy sessions later—at times after months—I am struck by my own preferred aesthetic. Alongside advice from my therapist and realizations that I want to hold on to are oil-pastel drawings of made-up plant species, surreally large pots and pebbles. It is a kind of futurist science fiction for the mental landscape I am moving towards. A writer I often turn to, Tiana Clark, told me, 'I am writing to save my own life first. If my work helps someone else, that's wonderful too.' The forest and nested words on the page in front of me read back to me that way: I am not trying to be creative in any conscious way in these moments. *I am trying to save my life.*

I am continually stumped by the fact that there exist sights and sounds that can stop me in my tracks—the sudden crop of needle-thin mushrooms in a flower pot one monsoon morning; a tiny red Pierrot butterfly holding fast to a petal in strong wind; the gradual appearance of thin, white roots on plant cuttings in jars of water. To my sister, I point out two large flies mating on the railing outside my window. She shakes her head in mild disgust—baffled by what I find compelling. Wonder is, in so many ways, the opposite of depression, the antidote to apathy. It is the defiant, resilient retraining of attention.

I am drawn at times, rather ridiculously, to admire the pigeon—the one that shreds my succulents and breaks the dishes in which I leave water for it in the summer months. A bird I have watched (and cursed) countless times, yet I am still surprised by the variations, by the particular image I haven't encountered yet. The way it transforms into an almost-white bird when it flies, evening light in tow. Pink claws clutching a white window rail. A dark silhouette shaking itself dry on the parapet in the monsoon. Late one evening, I saw the last pigeon of the day in the near dark on the balcony's edge, and I was struck by how the darkening blue quietened the sight of the bird, made it look almost spectral, like a sign.

～

If there is a form of writing I have found therapeutic to practise, it is the praise poem or the ode. That conscious composition is a way to record what moved me, what taught me, comforted me when the odds seemed unfairly stacked against me and others. In the throes of depression, cultivating gratitude feels counterintuitive. Depression kills the desire to seek out, to appreciate. I stop reaching for other feelings. At first glance, gratitude appears to come from the same reductive school of platitudes like 'thinking positively'. But the way I have learnt to wield it, through therapy and time, it is different from false positivity, in that it doesn't try to deny what is terrible (I *am* unwell) but it does allow me to recognize what calls for my respect, grudging or otherwise. It requires surrendering to both truths, a lifelong acceptance of the inherent contradictions of being unfortunate and fortunate at the same time.

I seek the outdoors because the natural world calms me. Some of my favourite sounds are the muffled soundscape of the ocean when I swim, the slight creaking of branches and leaves as a bird settles on a perch. 'Under the pines, the earth concocts/small unsullied things . . .' wrote Neruda in 'Ode to the Flowers of Datitla'.[2] I don't always write about every detail, every scene that piques my interest, but I hold on to them in my mind—I see that as a praise poem too. What I remember is part of who I am. The 'small unsullied things' of the earth have become my quiet conduits for repair.

I venture closest to understanding the appeal of recreational hunting when I go looking for birds—training the eye to survey long swathes of land for the right sort of movement that betrays the bird, the right silhouettes that press against the camouflage. It brings the attention to a single point, which happens so rarely and with little else, that I have begun to chase it.

I have been losing my mind spending weeks in a humid Goa, unable to perform the function for which I have taken time off from work—writing. I have internalized an unexpected and particularly upsetting work encounter. I seem unable to stop it from wearing me down. I stay in bed, unable to shake off the heaviness and irritability. I am upset over my inability to stem anxious and depressive thoughts about it. A friend reminds me, 'They should be the one racked with guilt, not you.' Though I understand and agree with her intellectually, I struggle to move past it at a more primal level. A different friend grimly announces that it is on me if I can't get over it.

One afternoon, at lunchtime, I make it outside and notice small birds flitting inside the firespike bush. I am captivated. At 1.30 every day after that, I find myself slipping out of bed and going outside, waiting for the sunbirds to arrive. After several days of trying to photograph these tiny, quick-winged birds who fly away at the slightest movement from me, I stop trying to do anything but observe. It takes some time for me to see past general details and notice differences among the birds, to recognize the blue metallic head and the dull olive one as a pair of male and female purple sunbirds. Through binoculars, over time, I notice and confirm a yellow underbelly on some of the male birds, so markedly different from the uniformly night-hued bodies of the others. It is a different species of sunbird altogether, no matter how similar it had seemed so far—a purple-rumped sunbird.

Watching the birds, I realize why I never saw the person's abusive behaviour coming. That's what's been eating me. *Why did I ever trust the man?* I believe in the evidence I am predisposed to believe, that I want to believe in: *Give me a polite person, with kind eyes, and I will cease to consider other evidence.* I will relegate their other acts of pettiness and cruelty to the periphery, slotted into the categories 'a small thing', and 'everyone is difficult in one way or another'. It takes me a while to notice what sets a thing apart from another. I pass off the malignant as benign over and over, as long as it is convenient, easier to do so—and who notices convenience as it serves them?

See how the repetitive attentiveness of observing the birds and learning their details relaxes the muscles of the mind enough to see what it has been missing. See how being quiet and merely watching will give one answers to the questions one hacks away at relentlessly without reward in the night. See how the shorn mental health comes together slowly again, how the birds dial everything in the body down to equilibrium, how one ceases to feel sad and thereafter stops asking if one is happy.

~

I walk around my residential area in NCR, picking different times of the day to see what else I can spot and hear. In this way, I find the local sunbirds before noon. Far less shy than the ones I encountered in Goa, they allow me to quietly film them drink from the purple flowers on the bauhinia tree. I have spent all these years thinking I live in a paved corner of the earth, and every walk proves me wrong. On a night walk, I find dark-brown snails exiting the grass on to the footpath, I swerve low to avoid bats that fly out unexpectedly from the sidewalk trees.

Slowing down and lingering offers me peace. It is a finite circle of the earth, but it continues to hold surprises—some mystical, like the appearance of an Egyptian vulture on the corner of the roof on a late March evening. I was so transfixed, I didn't even reach to take a photo or look about for my binoculars. If I had, I might have missed it take flight—revealing startlingly white wings edged with black.

Other surprises are smaller, quieter, like the brown underbelly of a kite that swims close to the building, the sprouting of new rain lily saplings from seeds I have collected from my plants. The surprise of finally spotting the white bands on house swifts on my evening walk—a detail I can't see when they're flying right outside my window: backlit, obscured.

I have become an evangelist for learning about one's local flora and fauna. I go on birdwatching adventures around and near the city with two of my closest friends—sometimes dazzlingly early on Sunday winter mornings, other times on too-hot afternoons, which at least two of us invariably regret. One of them talks too much for an activity like birding, consistently calls every brown bird a jungle murgi. Another confidently calls every small bird, no matter where we are, a tailorbird or a weaver bird—it is an endearing bias. Together, we misidentify almost everything.

I keep a log of birds and butterflies I see—on my walks, in other people's gardens, wherever I happen to go, even ones I see from the car (there's a plain tiger butterfly that I have seen on numerous occasions winding through traffic). Most I don't recognize when I first encounter them. I spend hours after I come home combing through my books, browsing on the net for images, calls, flight patterns and distribution. I am engrossed, and it takes me away from stale, cyclical thoughts.

There have been moments during depressive spells when I have stood intellectually aware that what is in front of me is astounding. But I haven't *felt* astonishment, haven't been moved. As I have become better versed in the natural world, I have simultaneously begun to gain more from each sighting, each variation, each new detail. The vocabulary allows for recognition, for a stake in what I am seeing. Now, even when I'm ill, there awakens a language in me, albeit weakly at first, when I enter my balcony, when I make it downstairs and to a park. I can step outside of myself and appreciate the breadth of the earth's gifts. *I see you. I see you.*

I can become overwhelmed with the tenacity of illness, the number of times it manages to rear its head after seemingly simmering down, by the baffling persistence of it. It helps to be taken outside of myself, for some part of me to be watching a pair of small birds on the grass, trying to notice identifying details, watching them hop for insects, bearing home memorized details, photographs and videos to identify them. When I get home, I am rendered anxious by minor interactions with family members—so little is needed for me to fall off course. I find out that the birds I have seen on the day's walk, hopping from bench to grass and back again, are

Indian robins (a male and a female pair). I write it down. It is enough to keep moving, to have something to move towards.

~

On my way, shortly before 9 a.m., to attend a talk on birds, I look out the car window. All I see are black drongos sitting on telephone wires. I have been depressed for days. Prolonged depression invariably crusts into anger. A friend has been unkind, impatient with my illness, and this detail rankles this particular morning. I want other birds to appear. Even the trusty cattle egrets casually perched on the backs of water buffaloes and cows are missing, and I am getting desperate, so I start to count my blessings that the drongos aren't crows.

I see a human couple on the way. As they lean into each other, I remind myself instinctively: *That is not necessarily for me, that is not guaranteed.* But up till the end, I will still be able to count the forked tails of the drongos, if not for anything else but to say thank you, thank you for everything I have that is not tied to another human.

~

## II

While a friend swims a quarter of a mile into the sea, her strong arms cutting cleanly through the surface, I sit in the small pools of water that have collected during high tide in the low-lying belts of the beach. The water is cold except for the radial area in which I sit, watching the tiny spherical button snails in the sand underwater sinking beneath the surface at the behest of their occupants. The sand plovers keep their distance from me as they hunt the tiny fish trapped in the pools till the next high tide unites the fish again with a sea of limitless escape.

Armed with a snorkel mask, I float for hours in the foot-deep shallows, where I can comb the sand for abandoned shells and dead coral. What holds my attention always feels like an awe-inspiring, undeserved present—those moments in which I clock into being alive at the right frequency, neither blunted nor too bright.

There is a window for peace, precariously proximate to the threshold for terror. I emerge above the water every few minutes to ensure I haven't drifted more than six feet from the shore or my companions. I strain my eyes on the wave-horizon to ensure I can still see my friend swimming, can see her in harmony with the current, can see she hasn't been carried away.

I think that if I verbalize being less afraid than I am, it will translate into real courage and capability. I swim after my friend into a rocky sea—flippers and snorkel on. For a while, everything is sanguine. But a series of strong waves cloud the clear waters. I lose sight of her, and a wave knocks my snorkelling equipment off. I know immediately that the odds are slim of continuing to successfully breathe as I panic in an unforgiving surge of sudden rough waves. I am swallowing water, and fast. It isn't that I don't know, somewhere in my mind, the science of surviving, but the panic consumes me. I scream and scream for my friend till she hears me. I almost cause her to go under when she reaches me and tries to lead me to a nearby rock—there is no shore close enough. When we reach the rock, I hold on to a portion of the rock as the waves continue to slam us against the rock face, the barnacles cutting our arms and legs as our bodies repeatedly hit the rock-side during the several minutes it takes for my panic attack to subside. This place, meditative in its shallow, unthreatening version, was nightmarish in a different avatar. The window for peace for my anxious mind is a narrow one, and sometimes, I have to bow down to fear, to not identify with courage I haven't honed yet—it is a muscle, and I am so early in the building.

### III

A convict named Michele Scott, who has gardened outside her prison cell for more than two decades, writes in an essay, 'What I do for plants is very different from how this place handles me.'[3] I am struck by her gentle, careful work in an ungentle, uncaring space, struck by the fact that she has given her years of imprisonment a nurturing frame. What I do for my plants is a primer, Scott makes me realize, on how to handle myself.

Over time, having become both more internal and more open among a small group of people, I have begun to squander time differently. I realized about a year ago that I needed a sphere outside of work, writing and people—some investment removed from verbal communication. I wanted to bring a piece of the outdoors home, introduce a small, fissured forest in the balcony where a colour continuum of yellows, browns and greens could eclipse the thick grey sky beyond it.

Part of this is remembering—I grew up surrounded by gardening. My father was obsessed with plants. I was impatient with it as a child. The chaos of the garden multiplying with new trees held little interest for me. But time and illness have changed me. What could better represent the practice of growing deep roots than a garden?

In the beginning, the old desire to identify and discourage disaster reigns strong. For the balcony garden, I need *hardy plants*, I stress upon the man in the neighbourhood nursery. I want as few as possible to die. 'None of these will die, right?' I keep asking him, and he keeps saying, 'No, not even one, not a single one.' I scribble his care instructions on a single yellow Post-it. The nursery is overrun by mongoose—the smell is disconcerting. I know nothing. As a start, I wash the smell off the pots when I get home.

Far from mother systems of soil and forest that have their invisible ways of keeping ecosystems alive, the pot-bound plants need additional care, labour, scrutiny. I struggle to keep up and learn their exacting personalities. Needs of nutrition, humidity, hydration and light met, the plants bloom, shrivel, burn overnight, produce seeds, push out new plants next to themselves from deep inside their roots, succumb mysteriously. I collect information feverishly from aunts, nursery men and women, the Internet.

For the first few weeks, I am convinced that every plant that loses leaves and stops flowering is on the brink of death. 'You're being very impatient,' says my father. 'They are fine,' says the gardener who visits once a week. The perennially flowering creeper that is on every gardening site's 'easy to grow' list stops producing buds after I bring it home, and more than a year later, it still will not bloom. I try every location in the balcony. The plants keep their own time, different from human rhythms. It is a kind of lesson—harsh and humbling—to not be able to control the plants' fate.

I kill so much before I learn a few steps of the dance that is being the keeper of a plant. Bit by bit, I am a better friend to them. When a Delhi summer of unrelenting 45-degree-Celsius days takes out a third of my plants in a week, I am ready to throw in the towel. My aunt's counsel: 'It is their first summer in your balcony.' This brings me back to trying—I know what a first summer is. On this path, in the garden, time is the single greatest ingredient. I grudgingly accept the cyclical—the long wait between blooms, the changing avatars of the plants with the seasons, even the dying.

'You're making a lot of effort,' my father notes, watching me comically haul a potted bougainvillea a couple of times every day into the few spots with sunlight as the clock turns the light. Of course, it is Sisyphean, and I must give the plant away to a house with an abundance of sun. I update him on what has perished, what has been culled, what I have replaced it with. I share that I am trying to grow tomato vines from seeds. He tells me the ones he tried to grow didn't make it. Mine don't either. We talk with a normalcy and a lack of tension that is largely absent between us. As I work on my garden vocabulary, one language forges another.

I arrive late to the identification of plant diseases, pests and weeds. Every part of the plant system, from root end to leaf tip, from the new unfurling leaf to soil, can catch a problem. No one warns me about the surprising beauty of certain weeds and garden snails. Slowly, I learn what health looks like for individual plants and how to help achieve it. Some problems I can't solve in time.

The plants anchor me. I worry about them when I am away. I ask my reluctant sister to send videos of the balcony whose audio I must turn down to cut off her commentary: 'Ew, ew, there's so much bird-shit, I can't be here much longer—' On days when I am too ill and cannot work, cannot be there for people, I still water the plants, clip away yellowing leaves and deadhead spent flowers, clear away the litterfall under each plant. There is always soil to be loosened and turned over. After meals, there are banana peels and tea leaves to be deposited as fertilizer. I play music on my phone while I move among the pots. If I don't pour water into the pots in time, the leaves droop dramatically. When it is difficult to get out of bed, I am grateful for the pull towards my plants.

When my grandfather visited, he carried Mexican petunias from the garden he fussed over with my grandmother in Bhubaneswar. It started with a single sapling carried in hand baggage on a flight. Mud had been caked into a ball around its roots and encased in a large leaf and tied in place for transit. Soon, I have a small colony of them. As they mature, the colour of their flower deepens from a pale mauve into a slightly unreal purple. The pots crowd with new shoots. Near the close of the monsoon, a few weeks after my grandfather, bringer of Mexican petunias, unexpectedly slips away, those plants produce seeds. The casing on the rain lilies, the only other plant in my balcony garden that has given me viable seeds, was thin. These seedpods are thick, made for durability and wind travel. Cracking them open, the tiniest seeds are found in both halves of the pod, which is edged with teeth-like fencing. I carefully wrap them in an old receipt and save them for my grandmother.

Because it is monsoon when he passes, the garden spills over every rim. There's no absence in the monsoon garden. I am here every morning, among the plants, because it is a way to be less futile, less lonely, less bereaved. I have never lost a healthy person before. Adding plants to the world feels like a suitable accruement, even though I know it isn't that simple. I have been thinking about my grandparents' garden since he passed—their care and the rich humidity of the eastern coast allowing for rows of roses, gerberas, allamanda, hibiscus, periwinkle and, of course, Mexican petunias. My grandmother's wanted a Malabar rhododendron for years, and we had finally managed to get her one a few months ago. Now, unable to live alone, she must move, must trade access to her garden for company, caretakers, ease. In place of humidity, she'll have to learn the many moods and complications of northern Indian climate. Whenever she is ready to start again, there will be saplings and cuttings from me—some grown from plants in her original garden.

~

# IN THE WEEDS

*On Mental Health in Virtual Spaces*

The utopian ideal of the internet—unregulated access to information, pure connectivity—now feels antiquated. Also antiquated: trying to determine if the internet is simply good or bad. Possible and necessary: thinking more deeply about how it is rewiring our brains and warping our experience of time, about the vistas of reality it is revealing and creating, and what to do with our positions therein, so that we do not go mad from it all nor flee altogether.

—Tavi Gevinson, *Rookie Mag*[1]

Among the last people I communicated with before I wrote these words are two friends I met online. One is launching the new phase of an incredible publishing venture, whose output I find consistently informative. One is a comrade in the winding alleys of illness, and we're talking about the most compassionate people we come across in public discourse. Whatever the costs of being online and available on various platforms have been, I have found and fortified ties there. It is a space that has both weakened and strengthened me, both bolstered my sense of community and fractured it.

When asked why she wasn't on any social media platforms, Ann Patchett told an interviewer, 'All I know is that there is not one extra minute in the day in which to communicate. It would be like knocking seven new doors into my house. I don't want to. Even if it would make some things easier. No More Doors.'[2]

We shape, the architecture of Patchett's sentiment suggests, if not the layout and size of our houses, then at least the number of additional doors. We start with a number of non-negotiable doors, doors we cannot shut for reasons of necessity, self-preservation, love. Patchett appears to say that it is not only our perceived idea of personal space we must protect but also the doorways, what we willingly neighbour. Each form of online communication I have adopted is a door I have knocked into my house.

~

What does communication in excess of what we can handle do to us, ask of us?

The convenience of communication—portable via our phones, reachability across a variety of mediums—dilutes or wholly wipes away the idea that we are doing our best. I fail people, constantly, by my inability to reply to each one and by my inability to do that within what people consider a reasonable time frame. I sit racked with guilt over these unfinished communications, over the angry or frustrated people on the other side. I see why letting them down is wrong, I see why writing each week to tell at least one person, 'I am terribly sorry, but I have been sick . . .' begins to undermine my words. I suspect at least some people do not believe me after a time. I understand that I would not either in their shoes—after all, the idea of sickness doesn't translate uniformly. *She has a cold, and she hasn't replied to me? She's always sick.*

We often have work to be done that depends on other people—work that keeps an organization running smoothly, the planning of a gathering or a coordinating of an urgent chore that requires other people to be responsive. I don't blame people for being disappointed by my delays. When the situation is reversed, I am disappointed by theirs. Seemingly, it isn't that difficult for me to reply, to update, to continue to participate in the back-and-forth till it is resolved.

I am grateful, in a preternaturally deep way, to those who say that they get it, they forgive me. I don't feel entitled to that understanding, I don't say this to condone the inconveniences I cause people. But the tools that each of us with a smartphone and an Internet connection have access to do not imbue us with equal powers. I have not become optimal at communicating in spite of the convenience built into these technologies.

I still expend the majority of my daily energy dealing with disturbances within myself and getting the bare minimum of personal and professional work done. The strings pulling at me outside of that add weight. It morphs from mild anxiety to full-throttle panic as a climbing number of messages and an increasing length of time since I received them make it psychologically harder to answer them. As Ashley C. Ford once suggested in a tweet, 'A permanent email vacation responder that just says "I am doing my best."'[3]

There's a famous moment in the movie *He's Just Not That Into You* (2009), where a character says:

> I miss the days when you had one phone number and one answering machine and that one answering machine has one cassette tape and that one cassette tape either had a message from a guy or it didn't . . . now you just have to go around checking all these different portals just to get rejected by seven different technologies.

What's funny at an intellectual level, but distressing at every other, is that despite being bad at communication outside my closest circles, I expect near-constant levels of contact from the ones closest to me. I have spent a disproportionate amount of energy seething over someone's inability to be there all the time—their phone is right next to them, right? If they can't be here physically, surely they should only be a message (and the length of time it takes to write a response) away? It doesn't matter that this logic is nonsensical when examined.

The warped, fear-scrounging parts of my illness will leap at every opportunity to tell me that the lack of a response can only mean that I am unloved or insufficiently loved. I have an innate tendency to believe that, and the illusion of the phone connecting me symbiotically to what is not physically present amplifies that. It ramps up the childish, the entitled, the most primitive parts of me to the point where messages—their perceived sincerity, depth of engagement and frequency—become a measure of love, without taking into consideration the other person's personality, schedule, health and circumstances.

One of my friends disappears off the radar and re-emerges when they feel able. I am accustomed to this habit—it doesn't dent our closeness. I still love them with a loyal intensity. Yet, I suspect I am able to do this because there are so many other people in my life who are consistently there. Once, I was hurt by a friend's lack of willingness to text more, call more—after all, we were and continue to be very close. After all, I *needed* them. They told me firmly, 'I will be a wreck if I do that. I need time away from my phone.' I had been asking my friend for what I believed was customary, the norm—all these other friends spoke all the time. I wasn't just somebody, I was important—so the rules of boundaries surely did not apply to me? It was sobering to be made to realize that I had been asking someone to compromise their mental well-being and make themselves more available to put Band-Aids over my own.

~

The fabric of my life, to hear me define it, would be woven through with the following threads: gardening, walking, reading, friends, family, partner, therapy, writing. In truth, I spend, as others do, a significant chunk of my day on my phone—consuming the details of hourly news updates, brawls that have broken out on social media, the minutiae of other people's lives, refreshing my email and then feeling paralysed by the need to reply. I don't seem to able to switch off from my follower count, my comments, other people's stories on Instagram. All of it feels like a powerful comment on my own life—that woman gardens better, she lives in the right city, she markets herself better, she is thinner, prettier, knows how to wear a saree, makes parenting look easy, has such a clean living space all the time. I don't put those impressions into words so much as I absorb them within myself as images— holograms that I'm reminded of when I'm dissatisfied with my own life. It takes a seed of doubt and grows it into a burgeoning tree.

The time I spend sunken in the world within my phone distances me from perspective and reality when it comes to the humans I love. It suggests other friends are closer, more effortlessly and loyally bound at the hip. It suggests friends are fonder of their other friends than they are of me. It suggests the romantic love that dares to declare itself on the Internet is the only real model, the only model that can stand up to unforgiving light and survive. It takes existing anxieties and insecurities and creates a movie of them. It becomes easy to interpret that the images I'm consuming are holding themselves to high standards of sincerity, that these are the only standards of sincerity that matter. The awareness that I am loved shrivels in the face of the solid certainty of other people's love.

There is a photographer I follow. Her professional photographs ultimately interest me less than her depiction of her family. She shares the highs and lows of motherhood, and that helps me follow along. A story with highs and lows is a more valuable and believable story to me than one that always ebbs upwards and beyond. Her marriage seems perfect, her children occasionally challenging but endlessly rewarding— an aspirational family by any definition.

There is a fact about both the highs and the lows that escapes me when I'm in the midst of a story served a few pieces at a time: it is arranged by a person whose fealty is not (and does not need to be) to the absolute truth. I am not just missing some details of her story. I know next to *nothing*. I only see her ironed, best clothes, her made-up face, her excellent eye for photographing her children with a professional camera. That's a strange thing to remind myself— it seems so obvious—but when one has been following along for years, when one is let in, one thinks that the passageway is a portal into that person's core, their life. When obstacles and frustrations are built into the stories I receive (and deliver), they begin to hold the sheen of truth for me. I have always been carried away by well-woven stories.

T. Kira Madden, a memoirist, extends this understanding of the portrayal of stories to non-fiction, 'They're still characters, I explained. The people in this book are not the people in my life. They are, and I am, projections.'[4] I think about this a great deal, because I have rarely read a book to completion without supplanting some portion of it dreamily on to my own life. I have compared, I have stored my impressions almost absent-mindedly into ledgers in my mind, placing the families I just read about in the category 'Variations on Families', placing the characters I just read about in the category 'Variations on Humans' and so on. Ann Patchett's mother read her daughter's novel based on their family and said, 'All of it is true, and none of it is true.'[5] The trouble, I believe, is that my mind sometimes can't tell that fatal difference when I am scrolling—speedily, lazily, without reflection. The truth is a chameleon; it is the story that's static.

I look around at the families that I know truly well, and none of them share the ethereal, luminous quality the photographer's family appears to possess. Yet, not all the families in my vicinity are bad. Some have strong ties they nurture consistently in a way that resembles families on the Internet, but I also see their restrictions; their shortcomings; their utter and human frustration with each other at moments; their concessions; their kindnesses to one another, which at times amaze me and other times set my teeth on edge. Other families are simply, heroically, making the best of being thrown with people whose characteristics make them particularly difficult to one another. Some organically fall away from each other.

The consumption of real-life variability and complexity is such a strange phenomenon, both validating our choices and making us wonder—what else is out there? Looking physically around me, at people I know, is an essential reminder that both tropes and variations run among us, as does mutability.

Our state of well-being is endlessly susceptible to manipulation by platforms, corporations and influencers who profit from keeping us in these spaces longer. The bottomless appetite for upgrades to every facet of my life—me, my work, my relationships—that these spaces foster has the effect of hollowing me out, leaving me more irritable, scattered and diverted by wants, which, if I were to take several steps back to see, are draconian in their expectations and discordant with who I believe I am.

Online, I have frustrated myself over not having what other people seem to have. It has led me to believe that neither I nor my career, nor even a loved one, is good enough or the right one for me. Jenny Odell, the writer behind *How to Do Nothing*, points out, '[W]hat we choose to notice and what we do not—are how we render reality for ourselves, and thus have a direct bearing on what we feel is possible at any given time.'[6] I have carried away catalysts for both depressive and anxious symptoms from my time scrolling. I have carried into my offline life the expectations moulded in a virtual world. Deep in the weeds of social networking sites, I have been missing that every aspiration (a healthy relationship, a redemption arc) must be adapted to the specific (chosen and unchosen) architecture of our lives. I am still learning that not every aspiration is additive, that sometimes to awaken want is to stoke dissatisfaction and an entitlement corrosive to myself.

~

Teju Cole said:

> [W]hat we're living in is the abolition of forgetting . . . the ability to forget is . . . part of what makes us human. You've had that experience of sitting on your computer and suddenly Facebook tells you something like, *A year ago blah blah blah,* and you're like, *Shut up*—you know?
>
> Or like the new iPhone says, *You have formed a new memory* . . . everything is crowding in on us. Everybody we've ever dated has a whole long email thread with them, every silly conversation we've had . . . an endless stream of photos—both ours and those of others.[7]

Google is fond of reminding me what I have searched for previously: a symptom, some guilty-pleasure celebrity gossip. When that happens, it is an unintentional, unchosen flashback. It is a small but pervasive invasion into our thoughts. We revisit the strangest, most inconsequential moments of our lives. We also revisit the moments we have wilfully put behind us, hopefully after doing the work of introspection and repair. Time is warped by our devices' ability to remember what we and others have fed into them, but which is not necessarily central to our lives—at least not any more. If I have typed it up, I no longer seem to determine its consequence. At times, a friend will send me a screenshot of an old conversation or I will send her one from an encounter I want help decoding. The noise of the present, though perilous, at least has the benefit of being the moment in which we happen to live. But the noise of the past, as our devices and the Internet remember it, is a heavily reduced and redacted reality. We switch gears within ourselves multiple times a day, an unfathomable number of times across the course of a lifetime. So much of the practice of being human is moving from one moment to the next. Much of the practice of managing illness is about riding the waves, waiting for symptoms to subside and the feeling of normalcy to return. It isn't the details of the past that weigh me down but the presence of it, as Cole says, 'crowding' me in. I don't want to live among our various redundant selves, the past casting a longer, clunkier shadow than necessary.

After a friend of mine crosses a busy, honking street, she stands on the side with her eyes screwed shut. I have seen her do this before—past a certain decibel, she loses her composure. She is physically rattled by noise. Silence, as the acoustic ecologist George Hempton defines it, is 'not the absence of sound, but the absence of noise'.[8] I am often reminded of my friend when I find myself thrown, when I find that I cannot proceed with my day because something has entered my stratosphere and disrupted what relative equilibrium I had. On my way to teach a workshop at a college, I received a nasty email. I opened it on my phone. It was from a friendly figure, and I didn't expect anything but a professional query. No one wants to be on their way to address a classroom when they receive an email that one has to read thrice before one can even comprehend that someone they know took the time to craft four hundred words of vitriol. I wanted to get off the train, to nurse the panic that was swiftly turning to nausea. I know some people who'd tell me to ignore it. However, we are not uniform in our ability to spring back from disturbances. I taught the class, saw a friend and went home—all the while feeling physically unwell from the email.

Unpleasantness is an unavoidable part of the human condition. But now the unpleasantness can reach me in more ways. There is a noise that comes with being easily available to the world—not merely the kind referred to above, but a pervasive din that leaves me standing often, as my friend does, by a busy road with my eyes screwed shut, trying to fumble towards balance.

~

My phone feels like a difficult family member sometimes, someone with whom I need to continually reinstitute my boundaries. I have observed the following around me: for a lot of people, when things get tough, really tough—they leave social media for a while, they uninstall one communications app or more. When my heart is breaking or I am navigating through a health crisis, social media doesn't help. It doesn't even distract, except badly, where scrolling is a restless activity that doesn't treat the unrest inside me and instead adds a layer of mental clutter, setting me back by time that could have better served building up a store of health or making progress on my to-do list.

Restraint and abstinence, by definition, open up space. As I stepped away from social networking platforms, deleting Facebook, uninstalling Twitter for long swathes of time, and Instagram on and off, I found an unhelpful variety of doubt recede. The more time I spend away from screens, the more I discover it is possible to live a life where I am not beholden to a constant loop of feedback that isn't my voice. In real time, I do not have the time and capacity to sift through that feedback to establish what I resonate with, what I should or should not be absorbing. Instead, when I am painting, assembling 500-piece puzzles, playing Scrabble without points with my sibling, cooking, gardening, talking to my friends, fostering my mental health, simply remembering to do nothing, I feel better, calmer—a feeling that I seek from my phone but never get.

Andrew Sullivan wrote of his detox from social media, 'The task was not to silence everything within my addled brain, but to introduce it to quiet, to perspective, to the fallow spaces I had once known where the mind and soul replenish.'[9] There is now space to notice when I'm starting to experience symptoms that require me to take care of myself.

Over the course of a day, where I was busy writing and stricken by panic, I approached my two breaks very differently. The first one I spent doing nothing, merely lying down, even getting a few minutes of sleep, and when I returned to writing, it flowed naturally. The second time, I just binged episodes of a show, which distracted me from my panic but didn't ultimately leave me feeling anything other than guilt over wasted time and scattered curiosity over the characters' fates: *Would they resolve that absurd romance?* I hadn't given my mind a chance to rest. I had redirected my attention, sapping energy. I was tired when I came back and wrote little; I had chosen a distraction, rewarding in immediate ways, over a replenishment.

Rohan Venkataramakrishnan, a journalist troubled by his compulsive phone use, found insight in *Hyperfocus* author Chris Bailey's work, 'Bailey argues that doing habitual, mechanical tasks—like folding clothes or playing an extremely simple game—does not take away from your ability to focus on something like a podcast, and is a far better reflex for compulsive multitaskers than checking Twitter, which does hog cognitive resources. Bailey makes the argument so convincingly that I even bought a fidget cube to reach for every time I'm stuck on a difficult sentence, instead of going for my phone.'[10]

With the help of quiet, I *listen* better to myself, I have more surface area to see the things that matter to me, hold my interest and, most importantly, keep me well. Sullivan described the experience of inhabiting quiet, screen-less time for the first time in years like this: 'My breathing slowed. My brain settled. My body became much more available to me. I could feel it digesting and sniffing, itching and pulsating. It was if my brain were moving away from the abstract and the distant toward the tangible and the near.'[11]

When I allow quiet places to thrive within me, I am more alive to the stimuli around me. I don't mean that I am willing to be swayed by every shift and about-turn in my radius, but I am cognizant of these changes. When a loved one is upset, I notice. When they direct anger towards me, I notice it, but more importantly, I am better able to defer my reaction till I have decided what response is warranted, and when, dependant on my own balance. When my sibling angers me with their carelessness, I am more likely to better engage with them when I'm not constantly comparing our story with the stories of other siblings I see on Instagram and Facebook. There is simply more room for the relationships in my life to exist naturally when I am less accustomed to hitting buttons to rid myself of feelings, when I am less accustomed to seeing human lives in constant relation to one another, and more centred as a result of spending more time by myself with longer tracts of time sans social media.

A friend asked me if I had seen the latest post outing a person in power's problematic behaviour. I hadn't—being on a long break from social networking sites. I read, and I followed, and I thought deeply about the relevant issues as a result. I felt tremendous guilt that I would be stepping away from a medium that brought so many people a place to voice their dissent, their experiences that wouldn't be heard elsewhere. I want to be part of their audience, but it does not have to be in real time. It wasn't simply the benefit of better health that kept me away, it was the fact that it made me listen better and speak more thoughtfully about the same issues I engaged with poorly when I was constantly plugged in.

~

When asked what the biggest contributors to her self-esteem had been, one of the things Gwyneth Paltrow named was 'sexual intimacy'. 'To be in that space, and to be who you really are, and not be judged for that, I think, that is a universal self-esteem builder.'[12] I am listening to her voice and the voice of the hosts, Dax Shepherd and Monica Padman, on the car ride towards my yoga class, and I know, in some way, that there are parts of this conversation I will remember, if not forever, then for a long time. The way I remember Rachel Noemi saying that the next phase of her life appeared to her only as she got to it.[13] The way I remember Sylvia Earle describing her ninety-year-old mother's reaction to her first-time scuba diving: *Why didn't you get me out here sooner?*[14] What I remember—sometimes without assigning an original thought to it or a proposed course of action—is an essential and primitive element of who I am, who I aspire to be.

There's an intimacy to podcasts, to radio, that I find unique to that medium alone. Music isn't quite the same, even though it does similarly wash over me. Over time, I have wanted less and less of social networking sites, which left me feeling tired, overwhelmed, unable to understand anyone, much less large human concerns. I wanted to understand, as much as possible, what has helped other people stay grounded, sane, rigorous in their empathy, what had allowed them to be good friends, family, partners and community members. In some way, I am always listening to stories with the view to understand where meaning lies, how health is meaningfully and intentionally achieved.

A digital-use application informs me that I use my phone four or five hours a day, that I pick it up, on average, about 150 times daily, that most of that time can be accounted for by social networking and messaging platforms. When I was a kid, I spent less time than that reading, and to hear me describe it, it would appear I had spent all my free time reading. I wasn't who I wanted to be any more. I have asked myself why I spend time on these sites. When I was posting, I was uncertain of what I was putting out into the world, but certain that I wanted to reach out into the world at that moment and make contact. I enjoy seeing the photos of my old professor's garden, the birds on my favourite ecologist's feed, the trees of my city chronicled painstakingly by one account. But among those simple, joy-giving desires lurks a reptilian curiosity about other people—a curiosity that wasn't driven by care but by the allure of spectatorship. I continued to give into that curiosity long after I had recognized it. I would finally step away after reaching a state of profound tiredness. What could I remember of those times? A smattering of details like a laundry list of who people had dated or not. What was that information to me? A small but addictive affirmation that I was *in the know*. How stupid such an affirmation might be was immaterial to how desirable it was. As widely established by social anthropologists, we have sustained a love through the ages for that widely available treasure that still feels finite and special to us: gossip.

I was filling my head (an already overtired, turbulent entity) with information that piqued a certain kind of interest, and it was leaving me feelingly increasingly unfulfilled. When gossip occupies the human terrain of face-to-face or one-on-one interactions with loved ones, it still has one humanizing factor in its favour—it is building something, however mired, between us. But the infiltration of other people's lives, for scraps of information, like watching a serial that aired several times a day, wasn't humanizing at all. It made me feel not only unwell but also less than real.

Chibundu Onuzo wrote of the phenomenon, 'Are our cravings for human connection really satisfied by social media? Are we not like hungry men told to make do with bubblegum instead of food? We simulate eating: we chew, we swallow saliva, we taste sweetness in our mouths—but our stomachs remain empty.'[15]

When I listen to podcasts that interview people and engage with their work and their lives with sincere and respectful curiosity, I am nearly always incredibly enriched by that experience. I want to grow, listen, take in, absorb, stay with a single person for an hour—an hour where I was not being sold either an item or an ideal, an hour where I was not manipulated towards a cliffhanger, an hour where I was moving the needle within me forward in some infinitesimal way. I could tell that I couldn't hear my thoughts inside social networking sites any more, I was paralysed by comparison and self-critique, and by a tiredness of the way people did not appear to be listening to one another. I got angry easily, dismissive even more easily. I did not seem to be listening.

I didn't want to be separated from the world, to be estranged from developments, people, thoughts. As I tuned into podcasts, and I did chores or nothing at all, I noticed not only what they were saying, but how they were saying it—the moments when someone pushed too hard on a question that someone clearly did not want to answer, the times when someone reciprocated curiosity, the times when they laughed or paused, the care they took over choosing their words. It made me pay attention to the differences in people's voices—a tuning into detail I haven't done in a while, like walking in the shallows and turning over every shell with genuine curiosity because they are all different. I was replicating the listening I was being exposed to. It was a 'now-long-gone high school, long calls with my friends in the evenings' kind of intimacy—humans interested in one another, who treat one another with attentiveness and care, are without exception the ones that I learn the most about connecting from. It was an intimacy I did not realize I had been missing.

I was drawn to social networks for the same reason I was drawn to late-night MSN Messenger in the mid-2000s. I wanted to be myself, to connect with people, and this didn't come easily to me in person. It was a world at a remove, it felt less scary. In the beginning, it gave me a community. I found friends, some of whom I stayed in touch with for years, and some of whom I'm still friends with. These friends have read my work, championed my writing, offered me support. They have taught me about mental health, writing, balance, relationships: the pillars of my life have been shaped by them. But what has survived of those relationships has moved to more personal modes of communication.

~

Ocean Vuong wrote, 'Here's/the room with everybody in it.'[16] Stepping into the more public platforms on my phone, I appear to enter the room Vuong is talking about. The room with so many people in it that it is exhilarating—until it is exhausting. When I step out of that room, the silence is frightening and full of the real pressures and obligations of life. I can't say I'm not tempted to stay where responsibility is a distant rumble, where the distance between me and the difficult people in my life feels greater. But in my clearest moments, I know to be submerged is to make myself sicker, and to not tend rigorously to my non-virtual life is to let a future version of myself down.

# AMMAHOOD

*On the Possibilities of*
*Parenting while Ill*

Imagine a family tree—ample-branched, full of offspring that proceed to beget their offspring. Imagine it is mine. Imagine every family member with a mental illness—recovered, relapsed or ongoing—has a red dot next to their name. Once each dot has been inked, the tree resembles a semal in February. Look downwards at the right-hand bottom corner to find my name—a stub. No children—biological or adopted. I have four nephews. Their names hang lower than mine on the tree. They are too young for red dots.

Imagine in five years, I will be ready to seriously consider bringing children into the world, on to this tree of ancestors and descendants. It may take fifteen to twenty years for my child to manifest serious signs of mental illness, should they have one.[1] I will be slightly older than my parents were when they found out I was severely depressed and anxious. I suspect that instead of a movement forward in time, it will feel like a surreal rerun, a weak collapsing at the knees.

∼

The red dots can be sorted into baskets—attention deficit disorder, major depressive disorder, anxiety disorder, rapidly cycling bipolar disorder, post-traumatic stress disorder, schizophrenia, alcoholism, narcotics addiction, personality disorders. Some of these disorders are one-time appearances in the long, mired history of my family. Most names fall into the first three baskets.

Understand I am more tired now than when I started this paragraph.

Understand that this is not a scientific exercise. Once, an aunt drew a similar tree to understand why her daughter's fears permeated every corner of their life. I am drawing this tree to acknowledge that illness is passed down with blood in biological families like mine. The same way women's bodies overheat on my mother's side, the same way weight gathers at the hips and thighs on my father's.

Whether my future children arrive biologically or not, or not at all, I want this tree to be drawn. Please do not misunderstand me. This tree is not a tragedy. I have mentally healthy cousins and aunts on this tree. I want the children to look at them and understand this: *lightning ambushes some people and not others*. I want the children to know that their mother, their aunt, their grandfather and great-aunts, their ancestors did not choose this. But we learnt to cope, though we learnt slowly. We learnt to survive as individuals and, in certain cases, as a family.

I want these children—wherever on the mental health spectrum they find themselves at various times—to know that we are here, we are still alive. We are ready to pass on what we know about negotiating the hands one might be dealt.

When I learn that the first of my friends—a close friend—
is pregnant, I cry. At the time, I am certain my tears are
happy ones. I am going to be a kind of aunt. The word
'aunt' reverberates inside me. I call my mother's inner circle
of friends *maasi*—a Hindi shorthand for any woman close
enough to count as my mother's sister. While I was growing
up, their lives offered a spectrum of possibilities for my
future. I followed two of them in studying literature, another
in turning to journalism and yet another in how devotedly
I read. This is the role I envisioned for myself in those first
hours after my friend breaks the news. But a lever soon turns
inside me. For the next few months, I am obsessed with this
question: What kind of parent would I be—wait, no, first—
do I even want to be one?

~

There is a story I hesitate to tell.

Several decades before I was born, one of my great-uncles
aged eighteen set out towards Bombay to become an actor.
On his way back, he disembarked a stop or two early from his
train and disappeared. For ten or twelve days, he could not be
found. He was finally tracked down wandering disoriented
in a nearby forest. His sister-in-law, who was one of the
first female doctors in the region, recognized something was
medically amiss and took him to doctors in the cities. There,
he was diagnosed as schizophrenic. But his father (my great-
grandfather) did not want to hear that his son was 'mad'.
My grand-uncle was engaged at the time, and his fiancée's
family found out. The fiancée's mother was nervous about

marrying her daughter to him, but her father was adamant that they honour their commitment. They were married, and my great-uncle—at my great-grandfather's discretion—did not receive any treatment.

The story goes that he spoke to himself throughout the day. He imagined voices and conspiracies against him. He was paranoid that people were betraying him. He wrote incomprehensible long letters to other people and himself. Most of the time, it was harmless enough for the family to live with. He had spells of lucidity. He even managed to travel on his own to visit relatives. His moods were unpredictable and erratic, occasionally even violent. These outbursts were particularly bad during his middle age—when the disease had progressed unchecked for some years and old age had not mellowed him yet.

When he left for Bombay, he was of sound mind by all accounts. He was eighteen when the tide turned. Typically, schizophrenia shows up at an early age in men. None of his six children developed schizophrenia. The general population is only at a 1 per cent risk of contracting the disease, whereas first-degree relatives of those with schizophrenia have been estimated to be at approximately six times that risk.[2]

In her autobiography, actor Mara Wilson has a conversation with her siblings where they realize her diagnosis of obsessive–compulsive disorder isn't that bad because going by their family's history—one grandparent with a personality disorder and one grandparent with bipolar disorder—it

could have been so much worse.[3] A relative, whose daily
life and relationships have been shattered time and time
again by their disorder, says to me through tears, 'At least
I get to have a conversation. If it were schizophrenia, it is
possible I wouldn't have the language or the wherewithal to
have this conversation.'

*It could have been worse.* I think those words from time
to time. I have a mood disorder that is kept in check through
medication, therapy and working from home. But before
I was in recovery, I was in pain so heightened I wanted to
die. I have walked home bent in half from work because I
am unable to stop crying. I have had anxiety attacks that
last hours, that leave the muscles around my chest sore for
weeks. I could have had it *worse.* That could still be how I
spend every waking moment. My child could have it *worse*—
unmanageable pain. It has taken a lot of practice for me to
remember in these moments that there was once a time when
I believed my illness to be unmanageable.

～

I can barely hold on when I see my family in pain.

Especially my sister. My heart expands to accommodate
all the sorrow I feel when she is in pain. Is this what it is like
to have a child? I cannot stand it a moment longer.

～

Take this with a pinch of salt. The secret to happy families,
I concluded early on, was potential parents taking a long

hard look at themselves before embarking on parenthood. They needed to examine, I thought, their naked need to have children and ask themselves: *Am I built for this? Am I built for the toughest caretaking scenarios? Am I capable of loving without guaranteed reward?*

This is a list of questions based on events in my life or the life of someone in my immediate circles.

Can I drive my child to the ER in the middle of the night at a safe speed, yet fast enough to ensure they receive the care they need?

Can I remember the route to different ERs for repeat trips because I do not want the night doctors to begin to recognize us?

Will I remember not to cry when the doctor in charge of the ER does not charge me for this middle-of-the-night trip?

If my co-parent chooses to take a break from taking care of the sick child, will I allow them that peace knowing that it is momentary?

If my child is diagnosed, will I be able to read and reread the manuals of their disorder without losing hope, without slamming the laptop shut?

If my child does not participate in their recovery effort, will I be able to change their mind?

Will I be able to recall (in time) that this is not about me?

If my child inspires pure, violent rage . . .

I am tired of feeling sorry I have these questions.

In *Lab Girl*, Hope Jahren is asked to stop taking psychiatric medicines—ones she has been on for years—during the first two trimesters of her pregnancy. In addition to challenging hormonal changes during pregnancy, she must contend with managing without her medication and the medication withdrawal that is a known trigger for mental health relapses.[4] Consequently, Jahren's bipolar disorder resurfaces, and she has to be hospitalized for weeks at a time until the advent of the third trimester allows her to return to her medication.[5]

The average pregnancy lasts forty weeks—a little over nine months. Some studies show a heightened risk of complications from taking common antidepressants[6] and antipsychotics[7] during pregnancy. This requires women who are on these medications to choose whether or not to go off these medicines for the duration of their pregnancy as well as the duration of their breastfeeding journey, based on potential risks and benefits for both the parent and the child. In consultation with their doctors, some women do choose to continue with medication. In these circumstances, doctors prescribe the safest ones.[8,9]

The period after pregnancy also leaves many parents vulnerable to postpartum depression, postpartum anxiety[10,11] and, in rare cases, postpartum psychosis[12,13] as a result of acute hormonal changes and sleep deprivation that affect the chemical balance of the brain.[14] Co-parents and partners can also suffer from postpartum depression and anxiety.[15] The risk of suffering from these disorders is found to be higher for those with previous experience of depression or a family history of depression, including postpartum depression.[16,17]

The benefits of finding supportive, knowledgeable doctors cannot be overstated as one navigates making complex choices. In an essay on parenting with mental illness, Anne Thériault shares that her psychiatrist shamed her for breastfeeding while on antidepressants, even though she and her family doctor had chosen a medication specifically known to be safe for nursing mothers.[18]

In the times I have not been on medication, I have been far more susceptible to depression and extreme anxiety. The most severe of my breakdowns in the last three years coincided with the times I stopped taking the medication or was transitioning from it. Consistently taking my medication with regular check-ins with doctors lifts my mood, lets me sleep and keeps me from worrying so profoundly that I'm rendered physically incapable of crossing streets or catching flights or responding to emails. Of course, the medication does not let me off the hook from having to practise discipline, self-care and therapy. Instead, it elevates me to a level where I can pursue a life.

These common risks associated with pregnancy and parenthood may loom large for me because of my pre-existing anxiety and depression. Though I am worried about these transient dangers, I have learnt the slow and hard way that knowledge and experience are fortifying, and prepare one for various outcomes.

~

For a long time, I wanted to be a mother. I wanted to share what I loved about the world with my children. I had so many stories I was saving for them—my grandmother's stories from the Valley of Flowers, the stories my mother had memorized from tapes. The story about the boy whose name no one could say was my favourite. I picked out three names that meant the world to me. Despite all its flaws, I have always loved certain aspects of family—the quiet reassurance of sleeping next to someone I trust, the comfort of laughing at the same story for the millionth time, the gratification of saying outrageous things to my grandmother to make her laugh.

When I was depressed and living in a new city, I would fantasize about a husband and kids during the autorickshaw ride home from work. I thought if I had a home with a family and a dog waiting for me at the end of that commute, I would be happy, that a new family unit would save me somehow. I thought mothering would bring me the joy and acceptance I had not found yet. I was stupid, yes. But what I really was, was desperate. I was dating a man I did not get along with. But we managed to stay together for a long time. One day, my mother cut through the bullshit to ask me, 'You think marrying this man will cure your depression? Marriage is not a solution to your problem.' She was right. The husband and kids were the fairy-tale route to recovery. And as I tried to figure it out on my own, I lost my desire for that family. It began to scare me. What if those daydreams were nonsense? I need frequent time alone to be well. What if the pressures of parenting made me sicker? What if being an ill parent meant being an absent one?

For me, energy is a finite resource—an endangered species, a small candle wick in a town with a lot of wind, a bottle of medicine whose bottom shines out quickly. I know from experience how easy it is to feel let down by family. Before recovery, I often felt disappointed by my parents. My illness accentuated holes inside me that I expected them to fill—especially my mother. I was—and continue to be at times—a kid with a bottomless need for affection and validation. I have a propensity for loneliness that never really goes away. 'Why isn't it enough,' my mother used to ask, 'that I make sure there is always food in the house, that you are always taken to the doctor when you are ill, that I remember to pick up deodorant when you run out? Why isn't that worth enough to you?' I know love, in part, is daily labour, drudgery, it is plain old 'fulfilling one's duties'. Love is my mother always doing the heavy lifting. Love is me always wanting more.

No matter how much incense I burn or how much therapy I attend, I continue to have bad days of feeling sad, irritable and despondent. I have days when I am worried to the point of just needing to lie down while telling myself that I will try again the next day. In the past, I have not been there for other people when they needed me on days that I needed to be alone. I frequently feel like a bad friend, sister, girlfriend, employee—because a sick day can creep up on me in ways that I cannot explain to them.

I do believe, after reading about other people's experiences of parenting with mental illness, that it is possible to swim through the challenges. Kay Redfield Jamison, a professor of psychiatry at the Johns Hopkins University School of Medicine, writes, 'The moulding of the circuitry of the brain, the formation of its pathways and connections, will remain throughout an individual's life a product of both inheritance and experiences derived from interactions with the world.'[19]

I can counter inheritance with experience. I cannot help the poor wiring inside myself beyond a point, but I can build around that a stronger scaffolding and alternate ways of thinking about that life. In some sense, I suspect those with lived experience of illness, and who are in some form of active recovery, are uniquely placed to support and empathize with their offspring. I don't believe they are 'better' placed, but illness has, in my case, expanded my cache of compassion. I am more empathetic to other people than I was before because I now have an acute awareness that only a fraction of another person's life is visible to me compared to the deep ocean under the surface that I cannot see.

Thériault saw that her son developed a capacity for sympathy and kinship by seeing his mother both struggle and do her best.[20] She has found that adaptations are available to her: 'I have learnt to be creative in how we have fun together—if I'm not up to leaving the apartment, we might build a couch fort and spend the morning in there reading and listening to music, or we might spend an hour trading increasingly silly versions of favourite fairy tales back and forth.'[21]

In an essay on navigating marriage and parenthood while battling both her own and her husband's mental illness, Maggie Ethridge shares that what helped her was educating herself on these disorders and the best practices for how to navigate one's relationships, pursue self-care in a disciplined manner and take care of basic needs such as sleep, a healthy diet and exercise.[22] None of this advice is fail-proof or necessarily easy to sustain, but then neither is the rest of dealing with mental illness.

～

If I do have a child, and you are that child and you are reading this, know that I have entered every lasting relationship with a significant degree of doubt. The doubt means I thought through bringing you home; it means I opened that door carefully. Know that illness cannot be wished away, but it can often be managed. Know that I am relieved to be with you on this journey. Know I come with baggage. Know that I will put it down and hold you as I tell you that a worthwhile existence is attainable and within your reach.

# ACKNOWLEDGEMENTS

Shreya Ila Anasuya for commissioning the essay 'When You are Very, Very Tired, You Can't Throw Your Tired Away', for *Skin Stories*. It was the piece of writing that started this project off.

Harsimran Gill for editing and publishing the essay that would become the first part of 'Buoyancy', in *Huffington Post India*.

Aditya Mani Jha for publishing the titular essay, 'No Straight Thing Was Ever Made', in *The Hindu BusinessLine's* Sunday magazine, *BLInk*. For believing in me enough to give me the opportunity to write this collection during his time at Penguin India, for being an audience safe enough to enable me to tell these stories.

Anushree Kaushal for being an understanding and enthusiastic editor, who made the essays stronger. Manasi Subramaniam for championing this collection in the final stretch. Rachita Raj and Ateendriya Gupta for their excellent copy-edits and proofreading. Kafeel, Nazaqat and the whole team at Manipal Technologies for typesetting.

Ahlawat Gunjan and Upasana Agarwal for designing and illustrating a cover that represents the essays.

⌒

The therapists and doctors who have helped me along the way for helping me rewrite chaos into a life. Access to psychiatrists, therapists and medication has been one of my greatest privileges and advantages on this journey. I wish these were not luxuries.

⌒

Sohini for reading an early version of these essays, for her thoughtful notes and for her friendship which is quiet and constant.

Madeleine for taking care of me, for reading an early version of these essays and guiding me through edits and for her love which is restorative.

Kavita for being there when these essays seemed beyond me, for patiently reading phone photographs of barely legible scribbles and rough notes that eventually became this book, for shaping the essays with empathy, encouragement and love. The period in which I drafted these essays was turbulent and, without her, I would not have found a way through.

Sharanya for being among the first to encourage me to write these essays, for reading an early version and for counsel in the moments when writing and publishing left me feeling exposed and inadequate.

Srinidhi for sending me some of the best advice I have ever received about the nature of doubt, for being consistently generous with her time, affection and wisdom and for the space she has held for the broken bits.

Aarti for the talks about nothing at all and everything all at once, for being a steadying force in the last few years and for the evenings of art and tea (and occasionally cocktails).

Sanjana for being there for me in both times of illness and health, for making me laugh and for being willing to frequently get lost with me.

Kirat for all the ways in which he makes it possible for me to grow, for the reading recommendations that gave the essays further depth, for helping edit bits and pieces the night before submission, for being a source of strength.

Sheebani for knowing and loving the most complicated parts of me, for being someone who will understand parts of these essays in a way no one else will and for the gift of shared decades.

Arnav for being as ridiculous as me.

Ankur for keeping my faith in connection intact during an ill time.

Natasha for all the decompression she provides, for all the ways in which I can relax and be myself around her and for all the lightness she brings to my life.

Saras for holding me close when I was at my lowest.

Twinkle Lal for allowing me to quote her, for the gift of her words.

Janet Thomas, Arpita, Ashwin, Joanita, Kavitha, Kumud and the rest of the cohort from my time at Deer Park Institute in Bir, Himachal Pradesh.

My sister, for reading some of these essays and offering her advice and for being my friend.

My aunts and cousins for an incredible openness about mental health.

My grandmother and aunts for teaching me how to garden.

My parents for love and support, for growing alongside me and for accepting what many parents might not have.

What this community and I create daily between one another is the life force that powers both my health and my writing.

～

# APPENDIX: RECOMMENDED READING

The writing I have listed is not necessarily directly related to mental illness or mental health. I have chosen to include the varied sources I drew comfort or lessons from as well as writing that challenged the sense that I was alone. Mental health doesn't exist in isolation. It changes everything it touches, and it touches everything. This gathering of literature is about recovery, coping, gratitude, community living, turning one's life around, wonder, suffering, empathy, reflection, keeping the faith and more. I would suggest reading a little about the book before picking it up to see if it is right for you.

Jenny Lawson: *Furiously Happy* (Essays)

Ellen Bass: *Like a Beggar* (Poetry)

Marilynne Robinson: *Home* (Fiction)

Ann Patchett: *Truth & Beauty* (Memoir)

Kim Addonizio: *Bukowski in a Sundress: Confessions from a Writing Life* (Essays)

Joan Didion: *The Year of Magical Thinking* and *Blue Nights* (Memoir)

Terese Marie Mailhot: *Heart Berries* (Memoir)

Scaachi Koul: *One Day We'll All Be Dead and None of This Will Matter* (Essays)

Gayathri Prabhu: *If I Had To Tell It Again* (Memoir)

Aimee Nezhukumatathil: *Lucky Fish* (Poetry)

Elizabeth Strout: *My Name Is Lucy Barton* (Fiction)

Ada Limón: *Bright Dead Things* and *The Carrying* (Poetry)

Emma Mitchell: *The Wild Remedy: 12 Months of Feeling Better in Nature* (Memoir)

Arthur W. Frank: *The Wounded Storyteller: Body, Illness, and Ethics* (Non-Fiction)

Jerry Pinto: *Em and the Big Hoom* (Fiction)

Bessel van der Kolk: *The Body Keeps the Score: Brain, Mind, and Body in the Healing of Trauma* (Non-Fiction)

Ross Gay: *The Book of Delights* (Essays)

Jane Kenyon: *Collected Poems* (Poetry)

Shreevatsa Nevatia: *How to Travel Light: My Memories of Madness and Melancholia* (Memoir)

Donika Kelly: *Bestiary* (Poetry)

Roz Chast: *Can't We Talk about Something More Pleasant?* (Graphic Non-Fiction)

Cheryl Strayed: *Tiny Beautiful Things: Advice on Love and Life from Dear Sugar* (Non-Fiction)

Carleen Brice: *Orange, Mint and Honey* (Fiction)

Gregory Boyle: *Tattoos on the Heart: The Power of Boundless Compassion* (Non-Fiction)

Sharon Olds: *The Dead and the Living* (Poetry)

# NOTES

1. The quote from which the collection and the first essay borrow their title is from Immanuel Kant's *Idea for a Universal History with a Cosmopolitan Purpose* (1784).
2. *The Affair* is a TV series (2014–19) created by Sarah Treem and Hagai Levi and broadcast on Showtime.

## When You're Very, Very Tired, You Can't Throw Your Tired Away

1. The title is a response to a quote from a children's book by Ruth Krauss (illustrated by Maurice Sendak) called *Open House for Butterflies* (Harper & Row Publishers, 1960) that reads, 'If you're very, very tired, just throw your tired away.'

## Everything for This Beauty

1. Ioanna Carlsen, 'Fat' (poem), Poetry Foundation Website, 1991, https://www.poetryfoundation.org/poetrymagazine/browse?contentId=37995.

2. 'Everything You Need to Know about Antidepressants That Cause Weight Gain', Healthline.com, https://www.healthline.com/health/antidepressants-that-cause-weight-gain#ssris.

3. This sentence was inspired by the title of Kaveh Akbar's poem, 'Every Drunk Wants to Die Sober It Is How We Beat The Game', *Tin House*, no. 71, https://tinhouse.com/every-drunk-wants-to-die-sober-its-how-we-beat-the-game/.

4. Ali Akbar Natiq's short stories in Urdu were translated by Ali Madeeh Hashmi and published by Penguin India as *What Will You Give For This Beauty?* (2015).

5. Carmen Maria Machado, 'Unruly, Adjective', Medium's Gay Mag, 10 April 2018, https://gay.medium.com/the-body-that-says-i-am-here-f21c9642d49c.

6. The ninth letter of Rainer Maria Rilke's *Letters to a Young Poet* (San Francisco: New World Library, 2010), p. 89.

## Two Deer in the Headlights

1. A 2017 documentary written and produced by Jennifer Brea on her struggle to be diagnosed and to manage the debilitating symptoms of chronic fatigue syndrome.

2. Alexandra Sifferlin, 'Divorce More Likely When Wife Falls Ill', *Time*, 1 May 2014, https://time.com/83486/divorce-is-more-likely-if-the-wife-not-the-husband-gets-sick/.

3. From the 15 November 2009 issue of *Cancer*, in which gender disparity in the rate of partner abandonment in patients with serious medical illness by Glantz M.J.,

Chamberlain M.C., Liu Q., Hsieh C.C., Edwards K.R., Van Horn A. and Recht L. was published.

4. Daniel Kahneman, 'Chapter 26: Prospect Theory', *Thinking Fast and Slow* (London: Penguin, 2012).

5. Ann Patchett, *Truth & Beauty: A Friendship* (New York: Harper Perennial, 2005), p. 38.

6. Katy Maxwell, 'Girl of The Earth', *Winter Girl* (Tumblr), https://heart-fools.tumblr.com/post/121094768429/at-some-point-growing-stopped-being-painful-and. I first encountered the quote in an illustration by the Tumblr account @demiiwhiffin: https://demiiwhiffin.tumblr.com/post/126761907062/from-girl-of-the-earth-by-katy-maxwell.

7. 'Crazy' is not a suitable word to describe people with mental health issues. I have included it in this instance because that is how I felt at the time, how I was socialized to think of inner turbulence.

8. Sylvia Plath, 'You're', *Poetry* magazine, https://www.poetryfoundation.org/poems/49010/youre.

9. Elizabeth Weil, 'Raising a Teenage Daughter' (with comments and corrections by Hannah W. Duane), *California Sunday Magazine*, 30 November 2017, https://story.californiasunday.com/raising-a-teenage-daughter.

## Buoyancy

1. The collection S and I first bonded over, *The Yale Anthology of Twentieth-Century French Poetry*, was edited by Mary Ann Caws and published by Yale University Press in 2004.

2.  Paige Cooper, 'Towards a Poetics of the NFL', *Popula*, 25 July 2018, https://popula.com/2018/07/25/towards-a-poetics-of-the-nfl/.

3.  Elizabeth Gilbert's interview with Krista Tippett, 'Choosing Curiosity Over Fear', *On Being with Krista Tippett* (podcast), 24 May 2018, https://onbeing.org/programs/elizabeth-gilbert-choosing-curiosity-over-fear-may2018/.

4.  Joshua Jennifer Espinoza's poem, 'You Do Not Have to Write the Best Poem in the World', https://joshuajenniferespinoza.com/post/170164992942/new-poem.

5.  'Mystery Before Mastery' was the name of a writing workshop the American poet Ross Gay conducted at the Palm Beach Poetry Festival in 2018, https://www.palmbeachpoetryfestival.org/workshop/2018-gay/. I was first made aware of Gay's advice to pursue mystery over mastery in one's art in a tweet by the American poet Danez Smith, who quoted Gay's words from an AWP panel: https://twitter.com/Danez_Smif/status/971828050034937857.

6.  National Poetry Month is an annual exercise undertaken in April by poets all over the world who strive to write a poem a day for the entirety of the month.

7.  Naomi Shihab Nye recounts this encounter in her *On Being* interview with Krista Tippett, https://onbeing.org/programs/naomi-shihab-nye-your-life-is-a-poem-mar2018/.

8.  The American poet Fatimah Asghar discussed writer's block in a series on tweets in November 2017, https://twitter.

com/asgharthegrouch/status/926101606176829441. Asghar is the author of the poetry collection *If They Come for Us* (New York: One World/Random House, 2018).

9. Anna Faherty, 'The enduring myth of the mad genius', Wellcome Collection, 3 May 2018, https://wellcome-collection.org/articles/Wt4D1yAAAABKzRgND; Judith Schlesinger, 'Creative Mythconceptions: A Closer Look at the Evidence for the "Mad Genius" Hypothesis', *Psychology of Aesthetics, Creativity, and the Arts*, Vol. 3, No. 2 (2009): 62–72, https://scottbarrykaufman. com/wp-content/uploads/2013/10/Schlesinger-2009.pdf.

10. Kay Redfield Jamison, *Night Falls Fast: Understanding Suicide* ((New York: Vintage Books, 2000), pp. 178–81.

11. Scott Barry Kaufman, 'The Real Link Between Creativity and Mental Illness', *Scientific American,* 3 October 2013, https://www.scientificamerican.com/page/about-scientific-american/.

12. Listicles and articles about the trope of the tortured artist are widely available online. I have included the following as an example. This by no means covers every or a majority of the instances; it is merely a starting point: James White, 'Suffering for Their Art: The Most Tortured Artists in Film History', 3 November 2014, https://www.empireonline.com/movies/features/tortured-artists-movies/.

13. Judith Schlesinger, 'Creative Mythconceptions: A Closer Look at the Evidence for the "Mad Genius" Hypothesis', *Psychology of Aesthetics, Creativity, and the Arts*, Vol. 3,

No. 2 (2009): 62–72, https://scottbarrykaufman.com/wp-content/uploads/2013/10/Schlesinger-2009.pdf.

14. 'Artists with Mental Illnesses', CNN.com, 9 March 2017, https://edition.cnn.com/2014/01/22/world/gallery/artists-with-mental-illnesses/index.html; 'Nine Famous Writers with Depression', Bustle.com, https://www.bustle.com/articles/90272-9- famous-writers-with-depression-from-sylvia-plath-to-jkrowling.

15. Judith Schlesinger, op. cit.

16. Ibid.

17. I first found *The Essential Rumi*, translated by Coleman Barks, in the excellent library of Deer Park Institute, Bir, Himachal Pradesh. The New Expanded Edition was published by Harper One in 2004. The poem, 'Buoyancy,' appears on p. 104.

18. Jessica Dore, 'November 2018 Tarot Offering', available on her website and sent to those who subscribe to her newsletter, https://www.jessicadore.com/november-2018-tarot-offering/.

19. Joan Didion, 'The White Album', *The White Album* (New York: Farrar, Straus and Giroux, 2009), p. 11.

20. From a tweet by Rachel McKibbens on 12 December 2018, https://mobile.twitter.com/RachelMcKibbens/status/1073023511973806081.

## Louder than the Music

1. Victoria Chang, *Barbie Chang* (Port Townsend, Washington: Copper Canyon Press, 2017).

## What Is Next Is What the Story Most Requires

1. The title of the essay is borrowed from a line in Jeff Hardin's poem, 'Concerning the Shape of Time', which can be read on Poets.org, https://poets.org/poem/concerning-shape-time.
2. Kay Redfield Jamison, op. cit.
3. Dylan Thomas, 'Do Not Go Gentle into That Good Night', Poets.org, https://poets.org/poem/do-not-go-gentle-good-night
4. Jennifer Michael Hecht, '10 things I wish people understood about suicide', Vox, 23 January 2015, https://www.vox.com/2015/1/23/7868621/suicide-help.
5. Gregory Howe Colt, 'Preface', *The Enigma of Suicide* (New York: Simon & Schuster, 1992), p. 12.
6. Kay Redfield Jamison, op. cit., p. 19.
7. Gregory Howe Colt, op. cit., p. 202.
8. Kay Redfield Jamison, op. cit., p. 7.
9. The line is excerpted from Chanda Feldman's poem, 'My Father Stands at the Mississippi River Bridge', which appears in her collection, *Approaching the Fields: Poems* (Louisiana: Louisiana State University Press, 2018).
10. Arthur W. Frank, 'Preface', *The Wounded Storyteller* (Chicago: University of Chicago Press, 2013), p. xi.
11. Jennifer Michael Hecht, *Stay: A History of Suicide and the Arguments Against It* (Connecticut: Yale University Press, 2013), p. 204.
12. Jennifer Michael Hecht, op. cit.
13. Anne Lamott, *Stitches* (New York: Riverhead Books, 2013).

14. Brene Brown, 'The Power of Vulnerability', TED Talks, June 2010, https://www.ted.com/talks/brene_brown_the_power_of_vulnerability/transcript.

15. Richard H. Seiden, 'Where Are They Now?: A Follow-up Study of Suicide Attempters from the Golden Gate Bridge', *Suicide and Life Threatening Behavior*, Vol. 8 (4) (Winter 1978), http://seattlefriends.org/files/seiden_study.pdf.

16. Robert Carroll, Chris Metcalfe and David Gunnel, 'Hospital Presenting Self-Harm and Risk of Fatal and Non-Fatal Repetition: Systematic Review and Meta-Analysis', PLOS ONE, 28 February 2014, https://journals.plos.org/plosone/article?id=10.1371/journal.pone.0089944.

17. Jeff Hardin, 'Concerning the Shape of Time', Poets.org, https://poets.org/poem/concerning-shape-time.

18. Gregory Boyle, 'Chapter One: God, I Guess', *Tattoos on the Heart: The Power of Boundless Compassion* (New York: Simon & Schuster, 2010).

19. The letter and Cheryl Strayed's response can be read at The Rumpus, where it was first published on 3 June 2010, https://therumpus.net/2010/06/dear-sugar-the-rumpus-advice-column-39-the-baby-bird/.

## Waiting for Sunbirds

1. Ross Gay, 'Sorrow Is Not My Name', Poetry Foundation, https://www.poetryfoundation.org/poems/92472/sorrow-is-not-my-name.

2. Pablo Neruda, *All the Odes: A Bilingual Edition*, ed. Ilan Stavans (New York: Farrar, Straus and Giroux, 2013).

3. Michele Scott, 'Doing Whatever It Takes to Create a Prison Garden', The Marshall Project, 9 June 2015, https://www.themarshallproject.org/2015/06/09/doing-whatever-it-takes-to-create-a-prison-garden.

## In the Weeds

1. Tavi Gevinson, 'Editor's Letter', *Rookie Mag*, January 2018 issue, theme 'Utopia', https://www.rookiemag.com/2018/01/editors-letter-75/.

2. Ann Patchett's interview with Mary Laura Philpott, 'Ann Patchett on Stealing Stories, Book Tours, and Staying Off Twitter', Literary Hub, 29 August 2016, https://lithub.com/ann-patchett-on-stealing-stories-book-tours-and-staying-off-twitter/.

3. Ashley C. Ford's tweet on 18 November 2018, https://twitter.com/ismashfizzle/status/1064383550043115520.

4. T. Kira Madden, 'Against Catharsis: Writing Is Not Therapy', Literary Hub, 22 March 2019, https://lithub.com/against-catharsis-writing-is-not-therapy/.

5. Ann Patchett's interview with Mary Laura Philpott, op. cit.

6. Jenny Odell, 'Introduction: Surviving Usefullness', *How to Do Nothing: Resisting the Attention Economy* (New York: Melville House, 2019).

7. Teju Cole's interview with Khalid Warsame, 'Teju Cole: "We are Made of All the Things We Have Consumed",' Literary Hub, 22 March 2018, https://lithub.com/teju-cole-we-are-made-of-all-the-things-we-have-consumed/.

8. 'Silence and the Presence of Everything', George Hempton's interview with Krista Tippett, *On Being*

*with Krista Tippett* (podcast), 10 May 2012, https://onbeing.org/programs/gordon-hempton-silence-and-the-presence-of-everything/.

9. Andrew Sullivan, 'I Used to Be a Human Being', *New York* magazine, 19 September 2016, http://nymag.com/intelligencer/2016/09/andrew-sullivan-my-distraction-sickness-and-yours.html.

10. Rohan Venkataramakrishnan, 'Worried about what social media is doing to your brain? This podcast has some answers', Scroll, 4 November 2018, https://scroll.in/article/900247/worried-about-what-social-media-is-doing-to-your-brain-this-podcast-has-some-answers.

11. Andrew Sullivan, op. cit.

12. Gwyneth Paltrow's interview with Dax Shepherd and Monica Padman, *Armchair Expert with Dax Shepherd* (podcast), 18 March 2019, https://armchairexpertpod.com/pods/gwyneth-paltrow.

13. Dr Rachel Naomi Remen's interview with Krista Tippett, 'The Difference between Fixing and Healing', *On Being with Krista Tippett* (podcast), 22 November 2018, https://onbeing.org/programs/rachel-naomi-remen-the-difference-between-fixing-and-healing-nov2018/.

14. Sylvia Earle's interview with Krista Tippett, 'Her Deepness', *On Being with Krista Tippett* (podcast), 7 June 2012, https://onbeing.org/programs/sylvia-earle-her-deepness-feb2018/.

15. Chibundu Onuzo, 'Social media mimics the intimacy we yearn for – but fails to deliver', *Guardian*, 9 March 2016, https://www.theguardian.com/commentisfree/2016/mar/09/facebook-social-media-intimacy-human-contact-craving.

16. Ocean Vuong, 'Someday I'll Love Ocean Vuong', *New Yorker*, 27 April 2015, https://www.newyorker.com/magazine/2015/05/04/someday-ill-love-ocean-vuong.

## Ammahood

1. Ronald C. Kessler, G. Paul Amminger, et al., 'Age of onset of mental disorders: A review of recent literature', *Current Opinion in Psychiatry* 20(4) (2007): pp. 359–64, https://doi.org/10.1097/YCO.0b013e32816ebc8c.
2. National Alliance on Mental Illness, https://www.nami.org/Learn-More/Mental-Health-Conditions/Schizophrenia.
3. Mara Wilson, *Where Am I Now?: True Stories of Girlhood and Accidental Fame* (New York: Penguin Books, 2006), p. 144.
4. 'Going Off Antidepressants', Harvard Health Publishing, 13 August 2018, https://www.health.harvard.edu/diseases-and-conditions/going-off-antidepressants.
5. Hope Jahren, *Lab Girl: A Story of Trees, Science and Love* (London: Fleet, 2017), pp. 276–77.
6. 'Making Sense of Antidepressants', Mind.org.uk, https://www.mind.org.uk/information-support/drugs-and-treatments/antidepressants/antidepressants-in-pregnancy/?o=7247#.XbkuHZpKg2w.
7. 'Making sense of antipsychotics', Mind.org.uk, https://www.mind.org.uk/information-support/drugs-and-treatments/antipsychotics/antipsychotics-in-pregnancy/#.Xbks35pKg2x.
8. Mayo Clinic Staff, 'Antidepressants: Safe during pregnancy?', Mayo Clinic, https://www.mayoclinic.org/

healthy-lifestyle/pregnancy-week-by-week/in-depth/
antidepressants/art-20046420.

9.  Jan Øystein Berle and Olav Spigset, 'Antidepressant
    Use During Breastfeeding', *Current Women's
    Health Reviews* 7(1) (2011): pp. 28–34, https://doi.
    org/10.2174/157340411794474784.

10. Melanie Santos ,'5 Things I Wish I Knew about
    Postpartum Anxiety before My Diagnosis', Healthline,
    23 April 2019,

11. Ibid., 'The bottom line', https://www.healthline.com/
    health/mental-health/postpartum-anxiety-what-to-
    know.

12. 'Postpartum psychosis', NHS.uk, https://www.healthline.com/
    health/mental-health/postpartum-anxiety-what-to-
    know#The-bottom-line.

13. Jennifer Marshall, 'What I Want You To Know About
    Postpartum Psychosis', *Bipolar Mom Life* (blog), 19
    September 2013, https://www.nhs.uk/conditions/post-
    partum-psychosis/.

14. 'Brochures and Fact Sheets', National Institute of Mental
    Health, Maryland, USA, http://bipolarmomlife.com/
    what-i-want-you-to-know-about-postpartum-psychosis/.

15. 'Postnatal depression', NHS.uk, https://www.nimh.nih.
    gov/health/publications/postpartum-depression-facts/
    index.shtml.

16. 'Brochures and Fact Sheets', National Institute of
    Mental Health, Maryland, USA, https://www.nhs.uk/
    conditions/post-natal-depression/.

17. 'Postpartum depression', Mayo Clinic, https://www.
    nimh.nih.gov/health/publications/postpartum-

depression-facts/index.shtml. https://www.mayoclinic.org/diseases-conditions/postpartum-depression/symptoms-causes/syc-20376617.

18. Anne Thériault, 'Mothering with Mental Illness', *Washington Post*, 12 August 2014, https://www.washingtonpost.com/news/parenting/wp/2014/08/12/mothering-with-mental-illness/.

19. Kay Redfield Jamison, op. cit., 183.

20. Anne Thériault, op. cit.

21. Ibid.

22. Maggie Ethridge, 'Living, loving, and parenting with mental illness', *Headspace* (blog), April 2017, https://www.headspace.com/blog/2017/04/30/loving-with-mental-illness/.